# DESTROYING THE POWER OF DELAY:

## Possessing Your Canaan

by

Sammy O. Joseph

Pulse Publishing House

© 2011  Sammy O. Joseph

First published 2004
Revised edition published 2011

Published in the United Kingdom by
Pulse Publishing House
Box 15129
Birmingham
England
B45 5DJ
*pulsepublishinghouse@harvestways.org*

*Cover design and typeset by Pulse Publishing House, England.*
*Printed in England* by Lightning Source UK Ltd.

**All rights reserved.** No part of this publication may be reproduced, stored in a retrieval system, or be transmitted, in any form, or by any means, mechanical, electronic, photocopying or otherwise without prior written consent of the publisher.

Bible quotes are from the King James Version of the Bible unless otherwise stated.

Amplified quotes are from the Amplified Bible, © copyright 1995 by The Zondervan Corporation and The Lockman Foundation.

**ISBN 978-0-9567298-1-1**

# Contents

| | |
|---|---|
| Acknowledgement | i |
| Dedication | ii |
| Preface | iii |
| 1. The Brevity of Life | 1 |
| 2. Destiny Detour | 13 |
| 3. Delay Exposé | 41 |
| 4. 22 Major Causes of Delay | 66 |
| 5. Deliverance from Inextricable Covenant Relationships | 89 |
| 6. The Four Clans of Giants en route Canaan | 126 |
| 7. How to Maximally Profit in Delay | 170 |
| 8. Overcoming Delays | 183 |
| 9. Virtues that Enable Maximal Profiting in Delay | 195 |
| 10. Make Peace with God: Possess Your Canaan | 210 |
| *References* | 212 |

## *Acknowledgement*

This book acknowledges two major personalities:

- the person of the Holy Spirit Who inspired me, poured into my vessel the limitless riches of His grace, and eventually encouraged me, not relenting His comfort unto me that even I may be counted among those who are *"able to comfort them which are in any trouble,"* by the comfort wherewith I myself have been comforted by God; and also,

- those who are troubled on every side, yet love the Lord and are patiently awaiting their day of redemption: *"Look up, for your redemption is very near!"*

Additionally, the untiring efforts of Suzie Tatnell and Faye White paginating this book are most appreciated. My dear friend Bryn Davies did an excellent piece of work graphically, designing the back cover.

## *Dedication*

This book is dedicated to my beloved Gabriella, David, Daniel, Priscilla and Paul, our dear "apostle."

*You're the very best children any parents could ask for!*

# *Preface*

In September 2001 when the Lord instructed me to write another book, sequential to *"GIDEON: Releasing the Potentials Within You"* which had then just been released barely four months – and had been well sought for – I resented the idea of *"couching up"* to conduct a comprehensive research for yet another volume; let alone upon the topic – *"Destroying the Power of Delay!"*

At that time, I was not prepared for another major project; yet, somehow, I knew instinctively, deep within me, that I was being commissioned by Heaven to write again. Fortunately, I accepted the mandate to share with you on an unprecedented *silent* topic as this, so as to enamor God's saints *not* only with the wisdom to help them navigate away from delay, but empower them to rattle the kingdom of darkness, bind captivity captive and release the bound.

This *new* book is a revised edition of that first published in 2004. It is richer and more informative. Not only will *Destroying the Power of Delay: Possessing Your Canaan* ensure your release; it will set you in quick motion towards fulfilling your destiny at a *godly speed!* I say *godly speed* because one of the most lethal weapons Satan has craftily fashioned to discourage, dislocate, divert or completely destroy the christian's morale from fulfilling the God-called purpose for their existence, is the weapon of delay!

Spinning the loom from – and weaving my thoughts around – the Bible's greatest delay tragedy, with the circumstances surrounding that poignant story as reported in *Numbers 14*, I have attempted to draw out life-changing teachings that will *not* hurriedly depart from you for an entire lifetime!

Be warned therefore, you have in your very hands, a destiny-changing book!

Have a blessed reading.


Sammy Joseph
*Birmingham*
*England.*

## Chapter 1

# The Brevity of Life

*"So teach us to number our days, that we may apply our hearts unto wisdom."*
— *Prophet Moses*

I have a few friends who do not wear wristwatches! Their personal reasons for their un-keenness wearing a watch vary from the corrosive-impact the golden bracelets leave on their wrists, to the residual tight markings left by leather straps on wrists! Quite a few people react unfavorably with skin allergies to wearing wristwatches; very much unlike me.

Unmistakably, fine wristwatches are an ornament. They are thus, a part of an adornment of beauty. In this case, the watch serves a dual purpose: a time keeper-piece and an ornament of beauty! A former East African President was known to have *'donned'* two wristwatches at any given period of time. Could you imagine: one watch-piece, a wrist! At first, the President looked obsessed, much to the bewilderment of his fellow countrymen. One hand kept the *British GMT;* the other, the local time. His obsession however soon paid off! His regime was reportedly characterized by a remarkable efficiency and prosperity unparalleled in the history of that region of Africa. He had governed Kenya.

Globally, a watch or a clock serves a primary aim: time-keeping. Overall, time-keeper devices remind men that their loan of life on this side of the universe is short!

Moses, having witnessed God's mighty acts on the newly freed slaves from the harsh bondage of over four centuries, penned the entire ninetieth Psalm with the theme: *Teach Us to Number our Days.* Summarily, whether you like it or not, life is *very* short. In fact, two words from which our word *"brevity"* emerges summarize the encapsulating meaning of life. The worded phrase that summarizes what life entails is *"brief entity."*

Life is a *brief* entity we are privileged to briefly possess, this side of eternity!

## *Applying Our Hearts unto Wisdom*

The *seconds* hand on a watch for instance, never pauses. And though life is brief and short, yet, it is continuous. Hence, to make the best use of the gift called *life,* we require the utmost application of godly wisdom in our daily decision-making processes. Wisdom entails centering our lives upon the perfect will of God for us. Wisdom calls us to zealously press – and make advancements towards fulfilling our destinies in Christ, in good timing, and inevitably, in good style.

Old Moses' heart yearned for the swarming, oncoming eventual inheritors of the Promised Land to incline their hearts to savoring the days in their lives – whilst they enjoyed the lives in their days! He had prayed God to:

> *"Teach us to number our days that we may apply our hearts unto wisdom."*[1]

Understanding the entity called *life*, therefore, is in itself, a gravitating propensity towards wisdom.

## Few Apt Descriptions of 'Life'

Established is the fact that *life* is short. It is shorter than should be misused, ill-invested or abused. Let us therefore notice a few vivid descriptions of *life* from God's perspective:

1.) At birth, God calls life's 'jump starter' air-passage, *"a breath of life."*[2]

2.) As we wriggle out of infancy and the cradle, *life* is described as a *"fountain of life"* just springing forth.[3]

3.) Closely monitoring this fountain stage, are spasms of outburst of hormone-releases. The *Sun of Righteousness* initiates us unto an enterprise of enduring comeliness. Our looks, shapes and voices begin to assume maturity. New energy is released into our blood stream; new thinking into our heads. Prophet Samuel describes the prime of our youthful exuberance as: *"the tender grass springing out of the earth by clear shining after rain."*[4]

4.) A well directed productive life is likened to *a flower in its bloom*. This flower opens up unto and basks in the radiance of the noon day Sun.[5] This *flower* has attained the exultant height of fulfilled desires and aspirations of its youth. This is Man's glorious state. Apostle Peter testifies that: *"all flesh is as grass, and all the glory of Man as the flower of the grass."*

Hear it better rendered: *"All mortals are like grass; All their splendour, like the flower of the field."*[6]

5.) After a *span of zap*, man's abilities and zest begin to wane. David, by God's inspiration likens life as unto *"a shadow that passeth away."*[7] A shadow-length is directly proportional to the overhead Sun. The shadow is shortest when the sun is highest. When a shadow lengthens, well-known fact it is that the sun has begun preparing for its place of setting.[8]

How did Apostle Peter summarize his findings on *life*? He aptly compared *life* to grass and flower that fall away after the bloom:

*"The grass withereth and the flower thereof falleth away."*
1 Peter 1:24

Black, blonde, ginger – even redhead instinctively summoned a Congress at which a unanimous decision was made. They passed a motion to appear in a universal color of parade during the upcoming *"Winter Sports of Life"*; they all agreed to file out bright grey! Take it or leave it, this is your destination. Better rendered; may that be your crown-attainment in Jesus' name!

Having aptly described what *life* entails, I should describe succinctly what life is *not*; this I shall endeavor to do in the last chapter of this book.

## *Our Triggered Response to the Brevity of Life*

Times change. Values change. So also do people. One factor however has always remained constant: humans in their correct senses naturally react to the brevity of life. Do not sway for the lies and the deception of the devil! One of his trump cards exposed is his attempt to convince you that you have plenty of time to decide about a venture or do a thing. The enemy of your soul has you as a pawn in his manipulative hands whenever you have been made to *procrastinate*: that is, postponing today's decision or action further until tomorrow!

Be reminded, procrastination is *"a thief of time."* It is the devil's #1 Trump Card waved in the faces of bewildered, confused multitudes he has in the *"valley of decision."*[9] The Bible makes us understand that Satan, the devil, is the enemy, *the thief of your soul*. *"The thief cometh not, but for to steal, and to kill, and to destroy."*[10] The Lord Jesus Christ, however, is the Bishop of our Souls.[11] He emphatically re-assures:

> *"I am the good shepherd: the good shepherd giveth his life for the sheep."*
>
> John 10:11

If procrastination robs time and the devil robs the soul, then both are robbers of destiny. Every fiber in your muscle therefore, ought to trigger a response to the *brevity of life* if you are a sane human being!

Notice with me these perfectly normal reactions to the brevity of time:

- a young man has been notified to pick his business visa to the United States and *he hardly has a minute to spare;*

- the real estate/property agents have nullified somebody else's delayed full payment of an offer – and extended same offer to another, to pay for the vantage parcel of land by a deadline; *the latter aims at beating the deadline;*

- investments, buying and selling in the corporate world have always had *price and time/deadline allotments;*

- seating for examinations and admissions into any institution of learning from time immemorial had always been advertised to the public through the media with three most conspicuous factors : *date, time* and *venue.*

*Haven't you taken notice?*

Conversely, the jesting of a group of girlfriends abruptly terminated once one of them suddenly glanced at her watch. She jumped up as if she had been accidentally pinched by a pin – probably after a couple of hours' fruitless chat. Something deep within tells her a fraction of *her life* has been irrevocably lost. *But she had been triggered off; suddenly!*

Somehow, I have come to realize that God designed it so; that His ace creation, Man, should always – and peradventure he/she forgets – be suddenly jolted to the truth that they have an allotted time; like footballers on the field of play to either win or loose, in the game of life. Each person has an allotted time space to either impact or be perpetually imparted by others in a competitive world of discoveries; to either gain an admission into College or University or forfeit the golden opportunity of education to truancy, hooliganism, and running around! A guy maintains *his* rightful choice, to either approach a lady asking for her hands in marriage – after prayerfully seeking the face of God – or to let go, keeping mute. Someone else may decide to take a timely risk, investing talent, time or treasures in a positively resultant venture or redundantly stash up capital in an unstable, unpredictable world economy that could be disrupted by unknown, unexpected variables. One thing is certain: we live in an uncertain world in which time-related decisions must be made – and failure to make those decisions automatically authorizes time to effect such procrastination to our utmost regrettable and remorseful resentments.

## *Seasons and Expectations of Life*

Summarily, there are eight major seasons in any person's life; each composed approximately of a decade. Our responsibility it is to prayerfully and carefully watch for the manifestations of these seasons.

Do *not* let *your* season slip you by. While you eagerly await opportuned timings, you cannot afford to miss a *door of hope*, manifested!

Here, therefore, is the *Seasons and Expectations of Life* chart I have drawn up. It has been aptly presented based upon biblical models. It should serve as a milepost-checklist on your journey through life – and not be used as a judgmental yardstick of performance or achievement. I pray you find it adaptable and useful!

# Life's Expectations Chart

| Age | Season of Life | Accompanying Expectations of Life |
|---|---|---|
| 0-11 months | Delivery Season | A new born infant jerks, perks, yells and soon begins adapting to the new world. He feeds and sleeps most of the time! |
| 1-10 years | Imbibing Season | Baby begins studying and learning about his surroundings a great deal. He gradually changes into a child, imbibing from the environment much like a studious apprentice. Life's values morals and culture are indelibly molded into a child's destiny at this tender age. This is the foundation stage of *any* destiny. |
| 11-20 years | Self Discovery | Dangers and opportunities *will* camouflage and begin to stare the growing adult in the face.<br>This young person will find him/herself inhabiting a world of choices.<br>The growing adult discovers self; thus strongly wishes to assert and/or exercise independence.<br>Sometimes, the young adult may feel the loneliness in decision making.<br>Psychologists refer to people in this age-group as adolescents. |
| 21-30 years | Equipping Season | An adventurous spirit is born. A *star* is paving ways in the clouds for its rays to shine through the Celestine night's sky. Once his identity is discovered, the emerging adult trains and equips himself for a lifetime vocation. He is self-actualized. |
| 31-40 years | Enthronement Season | The age *30* spiritually symbolizes the enthronement of a destiny. It is a critical stage.<br>Satan and his cohorts watch for to stop, thwart or destroy a destiny – as it is *three* multiples of *10*. |

*The Brevity of Life*

Once successfully enthroned however, the star's brightness intensifies. Establishment, acquisitions, expansion and dominion sequentially follow. (Notice, breakthroughs first occur in the spiritual realm before actualization in the physical.)

| | | |
|---|---|---|
| *41-60 years* | *Delegation Season* | Intensive training of a crop of carefully chosen, faithful employees belonging to the incoming generation of leaders begins. *CEO* fully delegates duties and assume a supervisory role to the next generation of leaders. On the family front, children are married off: daughters are given in marriage and sons take wives.<br>Soon, grandchildren begin to arrive: you have become a Grandpa/Grandma. Transference of godly wisdom and expertise should be the hallmark of this precious season of life! |
| *61-70 years* | *Impartation Season* | Transferring the family's or Company's trade secrets or success tradition to the on-line leaders with a view to allowing them a participatory role commences. This allows for inevitable changes in styles: particularly the modernization of and improvement upon the existing landmarks.<br>Grandchildren are carefully, biblically and prayerfully groomed at this stage. |
| *71 & Above* | *Longing for Eternity* | A longing for eternity begins to set in! Man begins to look forward to another life more than this he had lived. (A crucial identity sign for the recognition of those who have wasted their youth is toiling at this stage of life!)<br>Godly people who have achieved this age bracket transfer covenant blessings to their children and grandchildren. They continuously tidy and pack their cases in readiness for the journey to eternity! |

Let us all face the fact: humans love – and are desirous of living meaningful, purposeful lives! Hence a goal-less life is a miscreant to the purpose of God creating humanity. Realize also, that somebody's destiny somewhere is tied to your manifestation as *the* heaven-sent answer; *solution,* or *angel* to their *issues*; this is an integral part of the essence of *life*!

> *"For we know that the whole creation groaneth and travaileth in pain together until now."*
> Roman 8:22

Show up; take a bold, re-assuring step into your destiny. This is what you were created for; thousands have been eagerly awaiting your arrival!

> *"For the earnest expectation of the creature waiteth for the manifestation of the sons of God."*
> Romans 8:19

*Will you oblige Heaven, today?*

## Man and Delays

Because of our drive towards achieving goals, reasonable people are always time conscious. Somehow, *something* keeps whispering into our inner ears: *Time is not your friend!* Hence, Man is a creation in a hurry.

We hate delays and/or disappointments.

A good majority of us however have come to know by experience or through the rumors of somebody else's story that delay somehow has come to visit our world; and probably been permitted to pitch his ugly tent with us, much as an unwanted visitor as he is. His tenure of residency however varies, from person to person, people to people, family to family – even nation to nation.

Rightly handed, delay had eventually always brought tremendous spiritual and physical blessings in retrospect; manhandled many woes.

Trust me, some day; delay *will* knock on your door. Or probably intrude your privacy. I believe you ought to be prepared to know how to respond to his obstructive gestures, anytime, anywhere, any day! This was the reason the Holy Spirit asked me to undertake this project. My aim is to help you learn how to maximally profit in and through your life's delays.

If you will practice my suggestions herewith shared, you will emerge abundantly blessed more than you can ask, think or imagine.

## *An achiever's Diary - Charles Lindberg; Aviation Explorer Pioneer*

Charles Lindberg became an American hero at the age of 25 after he made the first non-stop solo flight from New York to Paris in 1927 on his tiny silver monoplane called the *'Spirit of St. Louis.'* After his historic flight to Paris, 150 000 people greeted Lindberg on a London Stop.

He returned to America to begin a carrier promoting aviation around the States. Fame followed him on his goodwill tour to Mexico late 1927 where he had first met the U.S. Ambassador's daughter Anne Morrow whom he eventually married in 1929.

Lindberg (and his wife) traveled all over the world as pioneer aviation explorers, mapping air routes for the airline industry. Most of today's *Worlds' Air-routes* are credited to his efforts and labors!

In 1941, Lindberg resigned Air Corps Commission, found work as an adviser to Henry Ford, building warplanes at Willow Run – and as an airline consultant to fighter pilots in the Pacific.

In 1954, his *'Memoir of Famous Flight'* won the coveted Pulitzer Prize.

In his latter years, Charles Lindberg traveled with an eternal burden: desiring an urgent need for balance between technological advancement and environmental preservation. He believed the aviation technology of which he was a pioneer was partly responsible for the devastation of modern warfare and the degradation of the natural environment, endangered species, forests and vanishing tribal peoples.

He died August 26, 1974.

## Charles Lindberg's Life Chart Summary

| | |
|---|---|
| 1902 | Born February 4, 1902 in Detroit U.S.A. |
| 1923 | Did first solo flight. (Aged 21) |
| 1926 | Hired as an airmail pilot. (Aged 24) |
| 1927 | Flies Spirit of St. Louis alone across the Atlantic at Age 25 thus making a World Aviation history record! |
| 1927 | Travels to Mexico, first met his wife to be, Anne |

|  |  |
|---|---|
|  | Morrow. *(Aged 25+)* |
| *1929* | Married Anne Morrow. *(Aged 27)* |
| *1929* | Mapping World Air Routes, promoting the cause of aviation technology influencing lives of would be pilots. *(Aged 27- 39)* |
| *1954* | "Memoir of Famous Flight" wins the coveted Pulitzer Prize. *(Aged 52)* |
| *1954 - '74* | International Speaker on Aviation Pioneering and Environmental Protection. |
| *DIED* | August 26, 1974. *(Aged 72+)* |

# Chapter 2

# Destiny Detour

*"Neither murmur ye, as some of them also murmured, and were destroyed of the destroyer."*

*- Apostle Paul*

I have tried to explain to you how brief the entity called *life* is. However, it is very highly unlikely that you would ever be able to understand Moses' standout piece of literature in the ninetieth Psalm, without first having a firm grasp of the background events in our focus chapter, *Numbers 14*. Here, the subjects in our cast would detour, particularly at the very brinks of fulfilling destiny!

## *Background Events Preceding Numbers 14*

Divine timing had just struck zero! It was probably the very last day of the second year of their great emancipation from Pharaoh's Egypt *en-route* Canaan, the Land of Promise. They actually bordered on the brinks of Canaanland; according to their available compass of that time.

Moses, the great Prophet of God had recently turned 82. His was an automatic admission through the *"Winter Sports of Life"* stadium gates: he was wearing a conspicuous, all-grey head. Psychologists have opined that each strand of a person's grey hair represents a major lesson in the *School of Life*. Whether or not this is true, we are sure Moses' eyes had witnessed the terrific acts of the Almighty God these past two decades – in addition to that supernatural acts of salvation and deliverance he had experienced in his infancy, in the papyrus basket, drifting on the croc-infested River Nile.[1]

Today, Moses, reclined in his wooden chair, relished both the coolness of the Paran desert evening and the momentous memoirs of the fleeting eighty years.

*"How time flies?"* he must have mused to himself.

He patiently awaited Aaron's ushering in of the spies sent to espy Canaan since the past forty days. This evening marked their deadline to *return to base* and submit their findings. Tonight was *the* night. Expectation was rife. This triumphant night's news should precede an exultant calvry procession into Canaan early the next morning – thus leading the two million-plus emancipated slaves into entering into God's rest; *their* rest, their everlasting inheritance promised them by the God of Abraham, their fore-father!

The story is told in Numbers *Chapters 13* and *14* of the Holy Bible.

Ten out of twelve War Lieutenants gave a *'100% Definitive Invasion-Impossibility Report'* concerning the Land of Covenant:

> *"And they returned from searching the land after forty days.*
>
> *And they went and came to Moses, and to Aaron, and to all the congregation of the children of Israel, unto the wilderness of Paran, to Kadesh; and brought back word unto them, and unto all the congregation, and showed them fruit of the land.*
>
> *And they told him and said, We came unto the land whither thou sentest us, and surely it floweth with milk and honey; and this is the fruit of it.*
>
> *Nevertheless the people be strong that dwell in the land, and the cities are walled, and very great: and moreover we saw the children of Anak there.*
>
> *The Amalekites dwell in the land of the south: and the Hittites, and the Jebusites, and the Amorites, dwell in the mountains: and the Canaanites dwell by the sea, and the coast of Jordan.*
>
> Numbers 13:25-29

It was a mutiny consensus report connived by the majority evil geniuses in the Wilderness Israeli handpicked *Lower House of Parliament*. This report startled their other two comrades; Representatives Caleb and Joshua. They were rooted to the spot in shock and disbelief of that which their ears had just caught. Caleb and Joshua seemed to have been naive of the fact that holding the truth captive had been with us humans, way back as early as shortly after the first couple inhabited the Garden of Eden. Anyway, their first reaction was to fight to liberate the truth, now obviously gagged and suppressed:

> *"And Caleb stilled the people before Moses, and said, Let us go up at once and possess it; for we are well able to overcome it."*
>
> Numbers 13:30

*Destiny Detour*

That is the certainty ring-tone in the voice of any overcomer! Overcomers' voices always ring positivity.

*Are you an overcomer?*

*But what happens when two strongest voices of protest for a positive change are muffled by ten loud dissenting voices?*

At the moment, a pungent smell of thick hostility pervaded the air. Any *nose* could smell it. That solemn statement of faith corroborating the truth had so suddenly portrayed Caleb and Joshua before the angry mob as an over zealous duo, insensitive and irresponsive to issues of the safety of their dependants' lives.

To the misinformed crowd, Caleb and Joshua sounded war-mongering. They looked a couple of trigger-happy – or should I rather say, sword-happy military brats! Confusion and uproar broke out in the Camp of the Congregation of Israel. The ten notorious dissenting lieutenants only stoked the fire, re-fueling it thus:

> *"The land, through which we have gone to search it, is a land that eateth up the inhabitants thereof; and all the people that we saw in it are men of a great stature.*
>
> *And there we saw the giants, the sons of Anak, which come of the giants: and we were in our own sight as grasshoppers, and so we were in their sight."*
> Numbers 13:32-33

Uptight emotions and democratic feelings were let loose in the *democratic* Church in the Wilderness. *How unfortunate!* Please follow carefully these accounts:

> *"And all the congregation lifted up their voice, and cried; and the people wept that night.*
>
> *And all the children of Israel murmured against Moses and against Aaron: and the whole congregation said unto them, Would God that we had died in the land of Egypt! or would God we had died in this wilderness!*
>
> *And wherefore hath the LORD brought us unto this land, to fall by the sword, that our wives and our children should be a prey? Were it not better for us to return into Egypt?*
>
> *And they said one to another, Let us make a captain, and let us return into Egypt."*
>
> Numbers 14:1-4

The rebellious, dissenting, wayward, complacent generation steadied to eliminate the men of faith; they plotted Caleb's and Joshua's execution:

> *"And the congregation bade stone them with stones ..."*
>
> Numbers 14:10a

General Moses and High Priest Aaron had already fallen on their faces before God, in the presence of the uncontrollable crowd. This posture of prayer should hallmark a strong persuasive tool to the misinformed people to re-consider their unilateral decision to make a *U-turn* – and head back into Egypt. If God promises a *deal*, count it a *done-deal*. Retrogression is not in His will for His children![2]

Decoded by Heaven, both Priests' cries had taken on an intercessory note! Caleb and Joshua also had had their garments rent: a sign of penitence and deep mourning for a destiny detour, that was about to occur.

But God showed up in the magnificent dazzling brightness of His glory. Only His sudden intervention such as this could ensure the preservation of the two wrongly accused spies. The four godly intercessors, prostrate on their faces, had come to know God so well. But Moses also had come a long way in understanding the people he had shepherded. He knew certainly beyond every measure of doubt that since they had sore tempted and provoked God the past nine times; they would retrogress into Egypt, this last attempt.[3]

Even though God is merciful, *"slow to anger and great in power"*, He revenges. His revenges are not *cool*; He *"will take vengeance on his adversaries, and he reserveth wrath for his enemies."* He will never acquit the wicked![4] His hot anger would be kindled, in a watershed of delay, denial and destruction – starting with the mutineer-heads!

And this was the verdict the Judge of the Universe returned against the dissenters:

> *"Because all those men which have seen my glory, and my miracles, which I did in Egypt and in the wilderness, and have tempted me now these ten times, and have not hearkened to my voice.*
>
> *Surely they shall not see the land which I swear unto their fathers, neither shall any of them that provoked me see it."*
> Numbers 14:22-23

They died instantaneously!

*"And the men, which Moses sent to search the land, who returned, and made all the congregation to murmur against him, by bringing up a slander upon the land,*

*Even those men that did bring up the evil report upon the land, died by the plague before the LORD.*

*But Joshua the son of Nun, and Caleb the son of Jephunneh, which were of the men that went to search the land lived still."*

Numbers 14:36-37

## *The Mystery Surrounding #5 & #10*

In Heaven's numerals, while #5 symbolizes *the completeness of a soldier's quiver* or *fullness of God's grace* upon a life, venture or thing, #10 however symbolizes the double portion of God's grace available to men and women of understanding in the *"temporary trials and difficulties they are destined to encounter and overcome!"*

Abraham succumbed to Sarah's suggestion to go in unto her maid, Hagar, only in their *tenth year* of their sojourning in Canaan. In retrospect we all wished Father Abraham had been just a little bit more patient! Laban changed Jacob's wages, just *ten times* – and the Saints of God will be tested for *ten days* of severe tribulation in the book of Revelations, yet they will attain the victory in the end. [5]

*Are you currently encountering the un-usual trials and difficulties associated with the 10th week, month or year in your endeavors?*

Here's the key: even as you are sorely tried and tested; be rest assured in the availability of the double portion grace availed you through Christ. Navigating the *#10* is going to be a little tricky for folk who fail to arm themselves with this key understanding; much like the congregation in the Church in the Wilderness!

These emancipated Jews had progressively enjoyed un-inhibited *"grace of God"* in their journey onto Canaanland. But they kept provoking God. Their relationship with the Father was not a warm, congenial, flourishing one; it was just *the* tolerant type.

*Could it happen that a child of God walking in disobedience to the Father's will could still be granted un-merited favor by God?*

Yes; very much so! The obvious problem is that such a rocky relationship with the Holy Spirit will not be flowing and congenial. It will be dry; one of mere tolerance on God's part towards such a provoker-child of His.

*Are you provoking God judging by your daily conduct?*

Don't shrug – and pretend you *wouldn't* know! You have been admonished to carry out a routine inventory of your *very* life:

> *"Examine yourselves, whether ye be in the faith; prove your own selves. Know ye not your own selves, how that Jesus Christ is in you, except ye be reprobates?"*
> 2 Corinthians 13:5

The *"God of all grace"* as described by Apostle Peter would continue to restrain Himself from executing His wrath while being continually gracious unto the disobedient until their *season of grace* elapses. If you would carry out a self-appraisal on your doings, you will not be judged of God:

> *"For if we would judge ourselves, we should not be judged."*
> 1 Corinthians 11:31

## The Concept of God's Grace

Let me explain the concept of *"God's grace"* a little further with Jesus' invitation to the weary and heavy burdened in *Matthew 11:28-30*. The Lord had promised them His rest. The provision of Jesus' rest is an act of grace extended toward the world of a sinful mankind. Hence, grace is *"an undeserved, unmerited favor; an act of kindness extended to the undeserving or unqualified."*

*Now, do you recognize that once you accept the Lord's favor and enter into His rest, that grace automatically assumes a moderate price tag?*

The price tag attached to *grace* is obedience:

> *"Take my yoke upon you, and learn of me; for I am meek and lowly in heart: and ye shall find rest for your souls.*
>
> *For my yoke is easy, and my burden light."*

As we obey and follow the Lord in daily scriptural reading, prayer and meditation, we *find* more rest – and without doubt, more grace. Those who are unwilling to pay the price of *finding* their rest, therefore, should never expect to continually abound in grace. They are such as are daily frustrating the grace of God – and the best state a frustrater of God's grace would inevitably dwell is in *"a dry land."*[6]

*Their dry land?*

Frustration in life and destiny.

*Why?*

Because they have missed out on the mechanics of grace; the basics of which is simple obedience!

Thus, if you have entrusted your life unto the Lord but have continuously lived in disrepute to God's words, your *"grace account"* with God is fast approaching red! You already wear the *"cord of grace"* as a bow-tie. This is the cord St. Matthew calls *"yoke"* in his gospel – same which prophet Hoshea rightly referred to as *"ties of love."*[7] But you are fast approaching the end of that cord!

If you originated from the continent of Africa – or had visited the continent during the different major cultural celebrations, you would readily conceive the idea of an *Easter ram* wearing a long cord, tethered and moored to a pole or tree. The spiral-horned beast awaits its ugly day: usually the day preceding the festivities. Aware, as if prompted by instincts, this beast knows its end is near; it begins to be panicky and jumpy. It tries to run as if to pull away from its mooring or uproot the pole along, in its "merry-go-round" escape bid. But the more it gets hyperactive, the shorter the cord gets having being either tangled or wound round the circumference of the mooring. At this point, the erstwhile watchful eyes of the local butchers – with sharp knives in hands – masterfully focus on it for any glaring miscalculation on its part, and as soon as it is their chance, they tackle and take him out.

*May that not be your lot in Jesus' name!*

The victorious Christian must *not* expect to sign in for God's *'season of grace'* ticket. Rather, he voluntarily chooses to wear Jesus' yoke, follow and learn of Him.

Israel, in the wilderness on the other hand, had exhausted her *grace season* ticket at the very brinks of covenant materialization. She had signed for – exhausted and abused *nine* previous tickets. This *"tenth time,"* God will *not* blink in judgment!

The Lord *"longsuffering and of great mercy, forgiving iniquity and transgression"* must *not* be taken for a ride. His grace must not be predated upon. His grace is not free after all! Jesus Christ, God's only Son suffered the consequences of our sins, shed His blood and purchased this freedom for us through His death upon the Cross of Calvary. This precious truth comprising of the suffering, the shedding of the blood, the death, burial and triumphant resurrection of Jesus Christ is the foundation upon which Christianity is built.

Hence, any who chooses to either neglect the act of obedience to the Lord, or willfully takes advantage of God's grace is berating and insulting God's intelligence.

Some of you are currently engaged in terrible acts of sin; yet God's judgment hammer has not clamped down on you! Be thankful. But more, be thoughtful. You attend church service and be-smudge thin God's wrath with a fat 'tithe and offering' envelope. You smile to yourself, thinking God is giving you a nod to continue trans-navigating your pleasurable highway. Be assured that your next mile-post will read: *Destiny Detour, 500 Meters Ahead!* God's *hesitancy in grace* must be not mistaken for slackness. We are told that:

> *"The Lord is not slack concerning his promise, as some men count slackness; but is longsuffering to us-ward, not willing that any should perish, but that all should come to repentance."*
> 2 Peter 3:9

Stop frustrating the grace of God – and your very self.[8]

# *Michal, Saul's daughter Frustrated God's Grace*

*What does it mean to frustrate the grace of God?*

To answer this question, let us refer to a case-study that stands un-equaled in all of scriptures regarding frustrating the grace of God. The story is about Michal, Saul's Daughter, David's earliest wife recounted in 2 *Samuel 6:16-23:*

> *"And as the ark of the LORD came unto the city of David, Michal Saul's daughter looked through a window and saw king David leaping and dancing before the LORD; and she despised him in her heart.*
> 
> *And they brought in the ark of the LORD, and set it in his place, in the midst of the tabernacle that David had pitched for it: and David offered burnt offerings and peace offerings before the LORD.*
> 
> *And as soon as David had made an end of offering burnt offerings and peace offerings he blessed the people in the name of the LORD of hosts.*
> 
> *And he dealt among all the people, even among the whole multitude of Israel, as well to the women as men, to every one a cake of bread, and a good piece of flesh, and a flagon of wine. So all the people departed every one to his house.*
> 
> *Then David returned to bless his household. And Michal the daughter of Saul came out to meet David, and said, How glorious was the king of Israel to day, who uncovered himself today in the eyes of the handmaids of his servants as one of the vain fellows shamelessly uncovereth himself.*

> *And David said unto Michal, It was before the LORD, which chose me before thy father, and before all his house, to appoint me ruler over the people of the LORD, over Israel: therefore will I play before the LORD.*
>
> *And I will yet be more vile than thus, and will be base in mine own sight: and of the maid servants which thou hast spoken of, them shall I be had in honour.*
>
> *Therefore Michal the daughter of Saul had no child unto the day of her death."*

A glorious restoration was making an in-road back to destitute Israel. The Ark of God – symbolizing God's presence, which had earlier been captured by the Philistines had been released and sent towards its original place of rest. It was a joyous mood, generally for everyone, except Michal.[9] She would not come down from her lofty room to join in the joyous procession. Instead, she would however cast a narrow, peering look through a parting of the blinds to catch a glimpse of the sight the hard beatings of the drums and the loud blowing of the trumpets had produced. She may have been melancholy or depressed – or both, I may not be able to tell.

As her lenses gazed widely, her aperture locked onto the *Davidic dance routine*: the joyous king leading a procession of troupe which was leaping and dancing before the LORD of Hosts!

Michal's heart was outraged! The Bible confirms that her heart feeling of despising the Lord – and the anointed led to her everlasting barrenness!

We understand from Michal's life that the *spirit of despise* of the man of God is the spirit behind frustrating the grace of

God – and an eventual frustration in life and destiny. Michal made a sharp detour of her destiny.

Friend, if you do not want to make a detour of your destiny, here is a suggestive – but *not* exhaustive – list of what you must avoid:

1.) *Do not despise whatever/whoever God has approved.*

2.) *Do not despise godly preaching/sermons.*

3.) *Do not despise godly chastisement:*
Some people cannot endure godly chastisement before they had jettisoned the brethren, the local assembly or even "the faith." They usually end up un-fulfilled in life.

4.) *Do not despise godly prophecy:*
God's word warns us against despising godly prophecies!

5.) *Do not despise godly worship:*
Worship opens the floodgates of Heaven. Do not despise godly worship – even if it has to be sacrificial. (Sacrificial worship is that worship you still render to God in spite of your pain, sorrow or affliction!)

6.) *Do not despise godly dance:*
King David sets the tune in *Psalms 149:3*; he wrote: *"Let them praise his name in the dance."* God expects us to worship Him, dancing! This means that the American can worship God with *the* dance. The English can loosen up a bit and worship the Lord with *the* dance. The Japanese can worship Him with *the* dance, too. Inspirational worship, music and dance are universal – and biblical.

7.) *Do not despise your protective cover:*
A son/daughter solely arranged and funded their wedding, for instance. Now they want to despise their poor parent(s) by leaving them out of the ceremony, just to mainly serve retaliatory purposes. No, my dear, *honor* is the word. The Bible asks you to set apart all acrimony – and *"honor thy father and mother,"* irrespective![10]

Protégés be warned; despise not your masters! Trainees, despise *not* your mentors.

8.) *Do not despise small beginnings:*
Great ends always begin little; in fact, very undoubtedly little. Even if your breakthrough tarries, you must persevere and await your time of lifting:

*"Say all the days of my appointed time will I wait, till my change come."*
Job 14:14b

Prophet Habakkuk admonishes you to wait for the appointed time of your vision, though it tarries.[11]

9.) *Do not despise God's servants:*
Some people have visited a servant of God without taking with them a gift in appreciation of the anointed; particularly, when God has used this man or woman as a vessel of honor for your lifting, healing, restoration or connection to the top. Your ingratitude depicts the inverse proportion of the value you have placed on the anointing upon their lives.

A friend of mine had been afflicted by an un-diagnosable infirmity for forty years; she had been rushed to the hospital by an ambulance, at least once, monthly; on a modest average, since she was aged 2. Something had always moved about her upper chest and throat, threatening to choke and suffocate her very breath.

Again, at age 41, she had fallen ill in the middle of the night and had been taken by the ambulance and admitted, just overnight. She felt same huge, suffocating discomfort in her upper chest. Various tests were conducted and blood samples taken, all to no avail! Summarily, because of her complaints in the particular area, a laparoscopic examination was conducted. The medical expert decided she would undergo a laparoscopic operation in a reasonable waiting time of twelve weeks. Then, she made a specific prayer request to me, to stand with her in prayers, regarding her healing!

I knew that "this kind goes not except by fasting and prayer;" so I began to intercede before the Lord on her behalf. The Lord soon spoke: *"You will lay your hands upon her, and the demon will let go of her – and she will be forever healed of the infirmity!"* She rejoiced at that news – and an appointment was penned!

On the last day of 2010, as hands were laid upon her, I felt *virtue* leave my body just as Jesus had *felt*, at the healing of the woman with the issue of blood!

I announced to my friend: *"Do you know you're healed by the hands of God – and will never be unwell again?"*

Derisively she had retorted: *"Oh yeah; but do you know how many people are praying for me?"*

Instantaneously, like a new teacher in accessing a new classroom setting, I perceived her level of spiritual perception as *fairly* low!

When she went for the scheduled operation January 12, 2011, the doctors reportedly spotted a fresh patch of red-blood cells newer than the surrounding areas. Reportedly, they could not understand what had transpired within three months, but found no reasons at all to progress with the *op*. She had been in the all-clear ever since; glory to God!

Despising God's servants is *not* only in berating their looks, outlooks, or the correctness of their vernacular and grammar; when you withhold that which is met from them, you have berated them and the anointing they carry.

10.) *Do not despise helpers and their acts of kindness:*
When somebody renders you good but you return their goodness and kindness with evil; you have spread a net for your feet. An instance most common is with the cash-strapped new arrivals to foreign shores that have to be adopted into families or "accommodation spaces" pending their proper settlement in their new countries. Some lodgers had spited their hospitable hosts speaking evil of them or acting wrongly against their interests! Somehow, it had not gone well with them.

Learn from their errors.

11.) *Lastly, do not despise the Spirit of grace:*
Presuming to always know the ways of the Spirit or your claims to a higher spirituality, a wider experience or a larger exposure to things of the Spirit will bring stiffness,

coldness – and more often than thought – personality clashes with friends, work-colleagues or members of a cell group in a local church. Either sister Euodeas or Syntheche in the Philippian church must have been a bit *'stiff'!* The truth is that no spiritual *'heavy weight'* could pre-determine the pathways of the Spirit of God.[12]

## *Covenant Transfer*

When Michal had despised David in her heart, she had also despised God.

When David had returned home after the festivities of the day, the Bible says he *"returned home to bless his household."*[13] Even though Michal had been ear-marked for God's blessings earlier in the day, she would, under the influence of the *spirit of despise* - squeeze a lime in David's face:

> *"And Michal the daughter of Saul came out to meet David, and said how glorious was the king of Israel today, who uncovered himself today in the eyes of the handmaids of his servants, as one of the vain fellows shamelessly uncovereth himself."*

That statement was her un-doing! God transferred her fruitfulness – as a Queen – onto the hand-maidens in the palace courts whom she had so highly esteemed a little better than worms!

Hear God:

> *"And of the maidservants which thou hast spoken of, of them shall I be had in honour."*
> 
> 2 Samuel 6:22

*Destroying the Power of Delay*

Friend, beware! God *could* transfer His covenant away from a despiser of His grace. In other words, He could disinherit *'promisees'* – even as these Israelites had been disinherited when He had effectually breached His promise to their generation.

Beware of these three prominent conditions that will ensure a covenant breach:

1.) *Man breaches the covenant as to cause the need for amendment(s) to the covenant:*
God made a pre-historic covenant with Abraham, the Father of the Jewish nation of Israel to establish him and his future generations in Palestine. However, the new generation of leaders refused to acknowledge the God of covenant – or the terms of such a covenant. God grew angry and dis-inherited them, scattering them all over the face of the planet until the re-birth of Israel in May 1948.

God emphatically finger-pointed *"their fathers"* as the deliberate covenant breakers.[14]

Because of His plenteous mercy, however, God eschewed the good *Olive* for a season – though *she* be terribly hurt; until *the* season of grafting in of the wild olive branches (the Gentiles) is complete![15]

When the season of restoration of Israel shall be due, the prophecies of Jeremiah should then be fulfilled: a new covenant, God will make; for it is written:

> *"Behold the days come, saith the LORD, that I will make a new covenant with the house of Israel and with the house of Judah.*

*Not according to the covenant that I made with their fathers in the day that I took them by the hand to bring them out of the land of Egypt; which my covenant they brake, although I was an husband to them, saith the LORD."*

Jeremiah 31:31-32

2.) *Continued ignoring of God's warnings:*

*"Because all those men who have seen My glory, and My [miraculous] signs which I performed in Egypt and in the wilderness, yet have tested and proved me these ten times and have not heeded My voice."*

Numbers 14:22; AMP.

3.) *Explicit renunciation of the Covenant-Keeper God or the terms of the Covenant:*

*"Death and life are in the power of the tongue: and they that love it shall eat the fruit thereof."*

Proverbs 18:26

Words are powerful seeds that will ensure unfailing crop-harvests. Words will harvest plenty or lack, health or sickness, destruction or security.

Many have ruined their marriages by their lack of ability to tame their tongues. Many children's destinies have been severely impaired because of this *power of the tongues* of untamed and untrained parents/guardians. Bosses and employees can ruin each others' days and lives by ordinary mere words.

In the same way, the blessedness of the fruit of our relationship with God can be enriched, enhanced and improved by the rightful and creative uses of our tongues. Destructive word-seeds in a similar token will hamper our growth unto His likeness. Job's latter, greater-than-former end would *not* have materialized had the suffering man heeded the call of his departing wife to *"Curse God and die."*[16]

Again, God has *never* been the originator of a covenant break; rather, the fault has always been found with Man! And whenever there has been a covenant-breach with any, *a* manifestation of delay has always been evident.

Because of the hardness of some hearts, folk may be dis-inherited; covenant fulfillment, thus, transferred to the next generation. Notice, God's distinctive redemptive benevolence unto mankind: if a person falls short of the grace of God to inherit his/her portion, that person's *seed* would be deemed to redeem/recoup it. For instance, when Terah, Abraham's father failed to enter Canaanland, God automatically extended the intended covenant He had had in mind for Terah, unto Abraham.[17] We read:

> *"And I will establish my covenant between me and thee and thy seed after thee in their generations for an everlasting covenant, to be a God unto thee, and to thy seed after thee.*
>
> *And I will give unto thee and to thy seed after thee, the land wherein thou art a stranger, all the land of Canaan, for an everlasting possession; and I will be their God.*
>
> *And God said unto Abraham, Thou shalt keep my covenant therefore, thou, and thy seed after thee in their generations."*
> Genesis 17: 7-9

Like Terah transferring the call to possess Canaan unto his son, Abraham; David too would become "breached" – and thus transfer the covenant to build the Jerusalem temple unto his son, Solomon. Much as he was prepared and zealous to build the great temple, God restrained David because he had *"shed blood abundantly."*[18] In modern expression we would say: *"His hands were bloody; a bloody man he was indeed!"*

God's restraint of David building, thus achieving his destiny's aspiration was king David's greatest life's misfortune; second in comparison to the *Bathsheba-gate* scandal! He referred to this tragedy of God's breach, as *"my trouble."*[19] The *bloody king* was disinherited for his son, Solomon – whose name translated: the beloved of the Lord, *"a man of rest."*

> *"Behold, a son shall be born to thee, who shall be a man of rest; and I will be his father; and I will give him rest from all his enemies round about: for his name shall be Solomon and I will give peace and quietness unto Israel in his days.*
>
> *He shall build an house for my name: and he shall be my son, and I will be his father; and I will establish the throne of his kingdom over Israel for ever."*
>
> 1 Chronicles 22:9-10

*Are you a 'bloody' person?*

Now, the inheritors of a transferred covenant *must* themselves be strictly minded to comply with the *deeds of the covenant* inherited, or they, too, stand the risk of a further covenant-transfer to the next generation. Aware of this precious truth, king David had therefore strictly charged his erstwhile wise successor, *not* to mess around with God's grace! These were David's exact words:

> *"Then you will prosper if you are careful to keep and fulfill the statutes and ordinances with which the Lord charged Moses concerning Israel. Be strong and of good courage. Dread not and fear not; be not dismayed."*
>
> 1 Chronicles 22:13; AMP.

You see, a covenant-minded person carefully focuses on fulfilling their destiny. They guard against breaching the terms that guarantee their inheriting their promised lot. They are aware that both *covenant-breach* and *covenant-transfer* are concepts in destiny detour!

The tribe of Benjamin was the smallest tribe in Israel. She inherited this status because the Lord was forced to make a breach upon her – which consequently, imparted upon the whole Israeli nationhood. But the other tribes switched into a perseverance mode; they plunged into deep mourning for their breached, abhorrent, rascally little brother, *Ben*!

> *"And the people repented them for Benjamin, because that the LORD had made a breach in the tribes of Israel."*
>
> Judges 21:15

Hence, Benjamin narrowly escaped total extinction off Israel's map via God's deft move to *covenant-transfer* with that particular generation by engrafting the *'Jabesh-Gileaditish'* women into that tribe. This story is well illustrated in *Judges 19:21*. From this story, it is established that a persevering, erstwhile intercessory prayer will serve an intervention tool at ensuring the *"one tribe cut off from Israel this day"* be restored.[20]

*Have you a 'Benjamin' in your tribe?*

*Isn't this story of Benjamin's restoration, a watershed point of repentance for you who "this day" could afford to remain at peace despite having suffered a child, sibling, parent or loved one severed from you?*

National disasters, political reprisals, persecutions, ravages of war – and their devastating effects have together totaled up as the single largest severance factor, forcefully separating relatives. Pertinent to our discussion and of equal importance are strenuous, raging family feuds between siblings, or the bitter wrangling that usually accompanies divorcing parties – with children caught in the cross-fire exchanges about custodial and visitation rights!

Now, ostracizing family members, communal or national citizenry one from another is a cantankerous breach that could lead to deep wounds of un-imaginable proportions. God's perfect picture from the beginning is that of brothers and sisters – and family members dwelling together in unity.[21]

This still remains His everlasting covenant with Man:

*"Thy wife shall be as a fruitful vine by thine house: thy children like olive plants round about thy table."*
Psalms 128:3

Hear me, heed God: retaliating against a spouse by *holding out* love from children or rejecting those kids will haunt you, later in life! That is a defeatist move. Playing *games* with your children's emotions promising them and not fulfilling those promises will be to your regret in old age. If you want to avert these pitfalls, start by the pursuit of a right heart! Yes, you're hurting; but start by being positively *thoughtful!* Think about your loved ones always. Think about the family members you were torn away from; think fond memories with a heart of re-meeting again. This thought and willingness for a re-union will most likely lead you to write letters, draw cartoons of the good times you had shared together – if you're the talented artist – or record your thoughts of them electronically; even if these may not be sent to them at the time, or received by them. But you have started on a healing pathway – a *very* positive process of releasing wholesome healing!

As time goes on, you may find yourself saying a prayer for them; but you had commenced the whole process of lasting healing with a positive worthwhile thought.

Listen to what God says:

> *"For the waywardness of the thoughtless shall slay them, and the confidence of fools shall destroy them."*
> Proverbs 1:32, JPS. 22

If you will graduate from just a casual mentioning them in prayer unto interceding for your *breached* loved ones, you will experience un-inhibited flow of grace from the Throne-room of God – and there shall be a sure restoration of the "breached!" Rachel lamented the breach of her children: *"weeping for her children refused to be comforted for her children, because they were not."*[23]

God heard her cry and cut her a covenant of restoration:

> *"Thus saith the LORD; Refrain they voice from weeping and thine eyes from tears: for thy work shall be rewarded, saith the LORD; and they shall come again from the land of the enemy.*

*And there is hope in thine end, saith the LORD, that thy children shall come again to their own border."*

Jeremiah 31:16-17

A few years ago, a divorced *forty-eightyish* grand-mother – whom we shall call Janet, not her real name – had not heard from her daughter who emigrated overseas since she and her father divorced eight years earlier visited our ministries' office in Nigeria. Spinster daughter – Emily, not her true name, either – had been distressed and had left home following a feud with mother over her shameful and indiscrete dealings with various men.

At her wedding ceremony, neither parent nor Emily's two other siblings were invited; Emily couldn't care any lesser, according to Janet's accounts. She along with her husband – and a baby toddler now formed a nuclear family. And now, after almost a decade, Janet desires a re-union and a relationship with Emily – and her new family.

Sitting across my table and looking agitated, Janet requests me to pray. *"I would love you to pray, Reverend, for a healing and restoration of the relationship between Emily and I."*

In my characteristic smiling manner, I had narrated Rachel's story above to her. I concluded much to her dismay: *"Sister, you would be the one in particular whose voice God would want to hear most of all – and probably in the dead of the night!"*

*"I can't deny me sleep for a stupid naughty girl,"* snapped the jolly lady, unguarded; *"so far as it's well with my other children and myself!"*

Well, maybe Janet is reading this book – or not, I would not know. What I do certainly know is that it is the pinpointed finger of the devil that moves a person to be so selfish enough as to pray that evil should avert them for the next generation. This had been King Hezekiah's uncharacteristic wicked attitude after God had discovered his folly in that he'd exposed his palace and armory to the spies from Babylon.

When Prophet Isaiah interpreted the king's dismal action as a sign of future enslavement and spoiling of both his throne and seed, Hezekiah had said: *"That's pretty O.K. by me so far as there's peace and truth during my reign! That should be more than fine!"* The recuperating, selfish king had mortgaged his posterity by the utterance of a single sentence of irresponsibility and callousness![24]

A great portion of Christendom would instinctively pinpoint Manasseh as the wickedest king of Israel; but Manasseh was only unwinding, spinning and threading his father's weaver's beam, loom and shuttle!

## *Need for Breach-Menders*

As I approach the end of this chapter, I want you to understand the heartbeat of Father God for our dysfunctional, wicked and evil generation. There has never before existed a period of time as this that God requests *'breach-menders'* – that is, intercessors!

> *"And I sought for a man among them, that should make up the hedge, and stand in the gap before me for the land, that I should not destroy it: but I found none.*

*Therefore have I poured out mine indignation upon them; I have consumed them with the fire of my wrath: their own way have I recompensed upon their heads, saith the Lord GOD."*
                                                  Ezekiel 22:30-31

The original word rendered *'gap'* above is the same word as *'breach.'* A breach is the devil's attempt at overthrowing God's assurance to a person, a family or a people. Oh, that God would raise up within families, neighborhoods, cities, counties and countries, quality *breach-menders*.

Remember, it was Moses' and Aaron's breach-mending, bridge-building efforts that had resulted into the next generation of Israelites being empowered to inherit Canaan.

Whenever you find *the* resemblance of a breach in your business, family and friends; go right ahead and raise a bridge in the name of the Lord. Do not leave this to someone else to do!

## Chapter 3

# DELAY-Exposé

*"To every thing there is a season, and a time under the heaven."*
— *King Solomon*

The fact that *life* is continuous but very short ought to inspire your quest to attain set goals in perfect synchronization of time coupled with a sense of tastefulness. I have never read of the phrase "laid-back" in either the description or vocabulary of *any* achiever. Overcomers do *not* rest on their oars; rather, they passionately drive onwards, towards and forward, in order to achieve more – and more!

Moses, whose inner weakness had denied him the joy of being an early achiever when he had been forced into exile forty years backside of the desert prayed God:

*"O satisfy us early with thy mercy; that we may rejoice and be glad all our days."*

Psalms 90:14

The route that leads to destiny detour ensures that you either never possess your Canaan or arrive there behind schedule, fagged out, contrary to God's perfect will for your life.

In this chapter, I shall by the Holy Spirit's enablement attempt to shed enough light possible on the entity called *"delay."* You must possess *your* Canaan on schedule; this is the essence of this whole project in your hands.

The word *exposé* in this chapter's title: *DELAY-Exposé*, has been borrowed. A french verb already in the past participle, *'Delay Exposé'*, therefore shall unravel such questions as:

- *What is delay?*

- *What are delay's possible causes?*; and,

- *What are the resultant effects of delay upon a person?*

## *What is Delay?*

*Delay* may not be accurately easily defined since it is either felt or actually partaken of, most times. Like wind, we may only feel its movement. Or witness its impact. I shall however attempt to describe *delay* as derived from a portion of our study passage of *Numbers 14:21-25:*

> *"But as truly as I live, all the earth shall be filled with the glory of the LORD.*
>
> *Because all those men which have seen my glory, and my miracles, which I did in Egypt and in the wilderness, and have tempted me now these ten times, and have not hearkened to my voice;*

> *Surely they shall not see the land which I sware unto their fathers, neither shall any of them that provoked me see it:*
>
> *But my servant Caleb, because he had another spirit with him, and hath followed me fully, him will I bring into the land whereinto he went; and his seed shall possess it.*
>
> *(Now the Amalekites and the Canaanites dwelt in the valley.) Tomorrow turn you, and get you into the wilderness by the way of the Red Sea."*

From our text above, *delay* has such varied definitions as:

i.) *The breach of God's promise:*
Notice with me, please, that just because of the irrational acts of a few spurious *provocateurs*, God *may* breach His promise to an entire group; thus, triggering into effect, mass delay. This should surely affect the entire group!

Be careful who you hang around.

ii.) *The wastage of a vibrant economic workforce:*
Thousands of Israelis in their economic productive workforce age-group were wasted in the wilderness along with the aged; the aged who possessed invaluable wisdom that would have done them much good in Canaan.

> *"Say unto them, As truly as I live, saith the LORD, as ye have spoken in mine ears, so will I do to you:*
>
> *Your carcases shall fall in this wilderness; and all that were numbered of you, according to your whole number, from twenty years old and upward, which have murmured against me, And your children shall wander in the*

*wilderness forty years, and bear your whoredoms, until your carcases be wasted in the wilderness."*

verses 28-29, 33

Additionally, whenever an economy experiences *'brain drain'* and labor mismanagement, economic paralysis must inevitably result. Thus, when an economy becomes paralyzed, many a destiny will become stagnated and threatened.

*iii.) Delay is motion in reverse:*
Contrary to popular opinion, delay is *not* fulfilled only in stagnation. Rather, *delay* could also be described as *motion in reverse order!*

As was the experience of the Israelites, instead of progressively advancing into Canaan while they yet tottered at the very brinks of same, God ordered their retrogressing by the very way they had come: the way of the Red Sea.

> *"Tomorrow turn you and get you into the wilderness by the way of the Red Sea."*

Numbers 14:25

*iv.) Delay is revealed in restlessness, wander-some thoughts, adrift off covenant targets:*

- *Do you find yourself becoming restless, wander-some in thoughts, speech and actions?*

- *Do you toss and turn on the bed at night, unable to sleep into the wee hours of the morning?*

These aforementioned are serious stress symptoms! Stress is a dreaded enemy and a silent killer of thousands globally, yearly. Stress will inevitably cause you fatigue – which may result in high blood pressure and potential death before your time.

Be warned!

> *"And your children shall wander in the wilderness forty years, and bear your whoredoms, until your carcases be wasted in the wilderness."*
>
> Verse 33

Similarly, fear of failure could induce stress and cause people to be adrift off the course of covenant establishment. Take this: Abraham and Sarah – and their team of *Covenant Explorers* had started out from Panda-Aram until they came into *same* Canaan; they had actually *entered* into Canaan! Check out the account of *Genesis 12:5* if you are in any doubt! This entrance means that they had supposedly inevitably encountered the land's original earliest settlers.

*You thought that encounter would have been easy?*

Think again!

This confrontation with the giants had doused their zeal for conquest; Abraham was *not* prepared to settle here. Guess what he did; he merely passed through:

> *"And Abram passed through the land unto the place of Sichem, unto the plain of Moreh. And the Canaanite was then in the land."*
>
> Genesis 12:6

Thus, when a people have not been able to *conquer* a place, they merely *pass through*. This is the key unlocking the mystery behind a *wandering spirit*. Merely *passing through* indicates the presence of frustration in the "passer-bye." Permit me to dwell here for a little while, tracing further, Abraham's *wander-someness*! The scripture records:

> *"And he removed from thence unto a mountain on the east of Bethel, and pitched his tent, having Beth-el on the west, and Hai on the east …*
>
> *And Abram journeyed, going on still toward the south."*
> Genesis 12:8-9

May I emphatically say that life's pressures had made Abraham detour from the *'School of Faith'* and gotten him enrolled in the *'School of Life'; the school of hard knocks*. Truth is, anyone who chooses to be tutored by life's unpleasant teachers, rather than the Holy Spirit and the Word must necessarily bag *The Survival Mentality Certificate Honors Certificate.*

> *"I have said, Ye are gods; and all of you are children of the most High.*
>
> *But ye shall die like men, and fall like one of the princes."*
> Psalms 82:6-7

*SMC* certified holders can hardly be persuaded to hold on a little longer to possess their Canaan; they would prefer the path of least resistance. They would rather wander – wandering, going on still, towards their dis-inheritance.

There is a key word in *Genesis 12:8-9* worthy of notice by a keen eye, which summarily described the only vital ingredient Abram lacked at this junction in his life's journey. That word is *"still."* Abram at this time lacked the ability to be *"still."*

This suggests to me that despite God's appearance and His re-assurance to Abram to stay in the land to fight and confront the gigantic opposition that stared him in the face, he chose, rather, to opt for the path of least resistance! He journeyed *still*, towards the South.[1] Towards Egypt. He and his team were lured away from the place of covenant to a few wasted years of frustrated life-style engrossed in cover-up's!

Someday though, Abram summoned up courage to eventually re-trace his way up north; to the *very* place of his earlier departure: *"the place where his tent had been at the beginning"* (Genesis 13:3-4).

*Have you been adrift off course, lured away from the place of covenant; the place of your first love?*

I earnestly pray the Lord to restore you this very day you have read this timely message. Not until Abraham returned *"unto the place of the altar"* of his beginning did the Lord hear him.[2] In retrospect, Abram would publicly admit that he did indeed *"wander"* away part of his earlier years.[3]

*v.) Bearing the reproaches of the parents' transgressions:*
If God's sentence to the Israelites in the wilderness to detour was inclusive of age bracket as young as twenty years, and having detoured for forty years; then it is reasonable to conjecture that the oldest of the new generation inheriting Canaan would *not* be younger than

sixty years. Think of it: children have come to bear the reproaches and the effects of their parents' rebellion against God. This is one effect of iniquity![4]

*Is this not enough strong reason why godly children should stand in the gap for their parents' spiritual inaccuracies – and as a matter of spiritual urgency, checkmate their 'irregularities' and transgressions before they mature into iniquitous generational curses?*

*vi.) Satisfaction arriving late:*
The detouring Israelites were forty years and a few days behind God's scheduled walk of mere eleven days! Shouldn't we all pray as Moses had prayed:

> *"O satisfy us early with thy mercy; that we may rejoice and be glad all our days.*
>
> *Make us glad according to the days wherein thou hast afflicted us, and the years wherein we have seen evil."?*
> Psalm 90:14-15

*vii.) Deferment of hope:*
Prolonged delays could induce life threatening or heart related illnesses. *"Hope deferred maketh the heart sick."*[5] Many a renounced case of infirmity comparable to those of the *In-Patients'* at *Bethesda Poolside Hospital* could possibly have been advanced by delay. Their case-file review carried out by the *Great Physician* revealed the severest cases of: *"the impotent, the blind, the halt, and the withered"* (John 5:3).

Circulatory and pulmonary diseases: the likes of heart-attack/failure, paralysis and stroke have their traces linked to fatigued hopes and frustrated efforts.

*viii.) The perversion of the original use/intent of a thing:*
Mouths of mortals must profess the glory of the living God; *not* utter perversity or profanity. This was God's original intent creating the heart-mouth connection! The scripture warns: *"Keep thy heart with all diligence; for out of it are the issues of life. Put away from thee a forward mouth, and perverse lips put far from thee"* (Proverbs 4:23-24). Abuse is the resulting inevitable consequence of an original intent unrevealed.

As soon as their sodden hearts conceived of returning to Egypt, and their perverted lips uttered same, delay was unavoidable!

*"As truly as I live, saith the LORD, as ye have spoken in mine ears, so will I do to you."*
Numbers 14:28

The Almighty's pronouncement above was a *"just recompense of reward"* of their perverted warped thoughts and speeches.

Guard both your heart – and lips![6]

*ix.) Barrenness, fruitlessness or unproductivity:*
*Delay's* ugly face can be detected in a deviant *peek-a-boo* game he is playing with you when you experience barrenness, fruitlessness or unproductivity. God's perfect will for you is to prosper in all endeavors of life.[7] If you experience contrary to the expressed will of God, let faith be born in you today to *grow sturdy legs* on the Word of God – and from that vantage height, *"fight the good fight of faith."*[8]

For instance, if a womb originally ordained by God to nurture babies has never conceived and in the stead of nurturing the seed of her man, has started to grow fibroids or miscarry, the couple must both *grow sturdy legs* and fight *the* perversion. Similarly, a church's growth could be perverted, suffer stunted growth and vision miscarriages; the spiritual headship of such a church/ministry so likewise must *grow sturdy legs* – and through prayer, re-order their covenant rights to growth and increase in the name of the Lord!

The Bible confirms:

> "Christ hath redeemed us from the curse of the law, being made a curse for us: for it is written, cursed is every one that hangeth on a tree.
> Galatians 3:13

In Exodus 23:25-26 we read:

> "And ye shall serve the LORD your God, and he shall bless thy bread, and thy water; and I will take sickness away from the midst of thee.
>
> There shall nothing cast their young, nor be barren, in thy land: the number of thy days I will fulfill."

x.) When a diversionary thought, an in-discretionary forlorn look and a depletive flat speech are present:
Anyone who exhibits any of these traits should be positive that they have been visited by the arch-enemy, *delay*!

The Israelites hatched their thoughts into one distractive action:

> "And they said one to another, Let us make a captain, and let us return into Egypt."
> Numbers 14:4

*xi.) Delay results when a sect arises from a followership forming a mutiny group against their leader:*
The Israelites hatched a mutiny-replacement plot against their spiritual head; Moses, an arduous task that inevitably resulted in futility. As in a reverse order, the heads of the mutiny chiefs rolled instead of Moses'.

## Watch these little Foxes!

Little things do add up big – and little foxes do *indeed* devour the vineyard. Be warned of delay's intrusions at such occasions as:

- *When You are Behind the Wheel:*
A male driver has been caught up in a very heavy traffic downtown. He has an appointment to make in lesser than fifteen minutes. A stranger poked her face in the passenger window, and our driver-friend has got an accomplice. Soon, he's heavily influenced by this attractive, foxy-looking *ET*! A hitherto, perfectly sane driver suddenly began to tap his fingers and feet to soundless fox-trot tunes whistled by his *new* friend. Subsequently, he began to curse: it was obvious, *delay* had accosted him!

He cursed the route, the traffic lights – and the city wherein he resided. He even cursed the car he drove. His tongue-lashing didn't spare the Police and the paramedic team that cordoned off the roads in order to evacuate survivors in a car accident. Little did this man realize that the *fox* has started nibbling at his vineyard!

- *When You're at Home:*
This *extra-terrestrial*-foxy-looking being will insidiously creep into your home, un-invited! *Delay* will engage the

mother whether she is married or single. It will attempt to stifle her erstwhile efforts at producing meals on schedule. Husband at such a time as this needs exercise a great deal of caution on himself while not sparing the fox. It is my recommendation that *hubby* kills the *fox* by joining his wife in the kitchen – and lending a helpful hand. (Husbands, prove me on this and see if you wouldn't have a resultant blissful night! This is certainly the way love goes – and amazingly, the *fox*, too!)

- *When You're attending an Interview:*
A job interview – or an equally important scheduled interview is worth waiting for. And *wait* you must; in cool nerves, unperturbed, probably engaged, reading a book, magazine or other piece of interesting journal.

A friend of mine who lives in an African nation with poor relations with the West attended a visa interview at a *Western* embassy not quite long ago. The inner voice asked him to take with him a book to read. It so happened that the book proved to be the first basic contact needed to guarantee his breakthrough! As soon as the visa officer caught sight of the book, his interest was kindled. Conversations flowed freely as it emerged that the officer had long ago read same volume which had had a huge impact on him. The book was *"The Power of Positive Thinking"* by Norman Vincent Peale.

Possessing these relevant information pieces I am sharing with you – and applying them to your circumstances *must* inevitably guarantee your position at the top! What I hear Heaven ask me to pen for you, specifically at this time is: *Invest time; not spend time!*

Can I speak these words over your life?

> *Every delay you have suffered will translate into stepping stones of glory in the matchless name of Jesus Christ.*

But please invest time – and *not* spend it. Your destiny will be determined by your character. Your character's forerunner being your habit; *your* daily habit foreshadowed by your act, and your act preceded by a simple thought! Do *not* sit idle; take a thought today to make each minute of your gifted life count. Make *your* life compact, not porous!

> *"Whatsoever thy hand findeth to do, do it with thy might; for there is no work nor device, nor knowledge, nor wisdom, in the grave, whither thou goest."*
> Ecclesiastes 9:10

If you read while awaiting an interview for instance, you would have succeeded in flaunting before your interviewer – or anyone who cares to take notice – an innate quest for knowledge. Your demonstration of *who you are* can be summed up by the watchful, eagle-sharp vision of an intending employer/interviewer. The outcome of an interview may just about swing around that piece of literature in your hands.

My friend who had in his hands *The Power of Positive Thinking*, had a whole interview of thirty-five minutes spent discussing with the visa officer, the summary of the entire book. He'd also been asked how his strong beliefs in *the* faith and positive-thinking message would benefit the communities he wished to visit in the United Kingdom. Long story, short: he had intended a short stay but had received a five-year multiple entry permit.

## *Helpful Tips in Defining Who You are to Delay*

Once *delay* shows up at your door – or by your driver's side window, all you need do is define who you really are to him. You will overcome the curse and the sting of *delay* if you put into practice these suggestions:

- Do *not* become impatient in a *traffic hold up* like our driver-friend.

- Delay will reveal your true character; for instance, being forced to wait will expose how patient you are! Beware *not* to give a false account of yourself.

- Meal times *shall not* run according to schedule if you are just starters on the marriage race! I deliberately chose my words: *'shall not'*. (The man should get off the sofa – get into the kitchen, roll up his sleeves and help his wife. On purpose – or as a surprise, a spouse should take their spouse out for a meal and a treat, depending on their disposable income. For ladies, romance doesn't just begin on the bed alone. It more than often starts in her brain cells as she witnesses your devotion to "serve" and help her.)

- Do *not* stare into the blue, panicky and apprehensive, if you are awaiting an interview. Behold I have attempted to equip you with heavenly *modus operandi* tackling the *little foxes*: get a book on you to read.

- Do *not* misappropriate funds and precious time. Financial delays could result due to the misappropriation, mismanagement or lack of innovations in investment of either or both time, treasures, talents and opportunities. This is how *"riches certainly make themselves wings: they fly as away as an eagle toward heaven."*[9]

## *Define Yourself, Financially: Beware of General Financial Misappropriations*

If anyone could muster enough strength to define themselves financially, they necessarily must escape delay's gruesome fingers. This is because your attitude towards money – the symbol of the *"life in the flesh"* – summarily determines *your* entire life.

So, let us delve into some *financial defining*, here!

*i.) Beware of other people's money:*
   The possession of a wealth ill gotten or the diversion of public, corporate or family revenues into your wind must surely take the winds out of your sail. You have attracted a curse onto your *lot* much like magnets attract metals. Your covetousness must trouble your links of acquaintances as did Achan![10]

*ii.) Beware of false declarations:*
   False claims and declarations in Income Tax Returns to the HRM Revenue Services, or the misleading of the Benefit Agency or the Social Services through erroneous information pieces furnished them in your calculated attempt to *add* to you should certainly ensure that *you* diminish.

*iii.) Beware of the emoluments of the deceased:*
   Some callous senior officers or accountants in the *Treasury Cash Offices* divert the emoluments of deceased people into their private accounts. They falsify books and refuse to declare to the appropriate authorities the death of such. Remember: *"Wealth gotten by vanity shall diminish."*[11] You can never have true lasting success, cutting corners!

*iv.) Beware of tampering with utility meters:*
Some drivers tamper with their cabs' meters to ensure more £ and *gains* over both the unsuspecting tourist and actual distance covered. You will later incur much *pain.*

Household energy consumers alter public utility meters or readings fixed at their addresses so as to pay lesser than the actual readings and units consumed. You have brought in a *fox* to rear as a pet! *"Ye have sown much, and bring in little; ye eat, but ye have not enough; ye drink, but ye are not filled with drink; ye clothe you, but there is none warm; and he that earneth wages, earneth wages to put it into a bag with holes.*[12] Because you have cheated; now, you will be *'scalped'*! You sow the wind but reap the whirlwind![13]

*Do you know a trader or a sole-proprietor who has re-shaped the standard measuring scales and altered the meters to cheat unsuspecting customers?* Assure them that they will be cheated too, on a grander scale than they have defrauded.

*v.) Lending out on usury:*
If you have borrowed money with a hidden intent of never re-paying, there will be no mercy shown to your generations.

Or you probably have lent money out on an unaffordably high interest rate; the Word of God condemns usury.[14]

*What does this ancient term 'usury' mean?*

It is rather interesting to note that the word *'usury'* has been derived from the primary root word *'use.'* No wonder, 'users,' 'abusers' – (that is, abnormal users of people or things); and *'user-dumpers';* I coined that term to describe people who have abused and dumped their victims – have always suffered untold hardship, in retrospect. Their retribution more than often times had been delayed unto the time they had well forgotten the evil they had earlier perpetrated. When *just rolling down their sleeves* to settle down and relax in life, they are suddenly rattled! Since they had *broken* other people's hearts, their hearts are *ground to powder!*[15]

No other instance is this accursed practice of "using people" prevalent than when a new settler enters a new country – and has been accommodated by a friendly family. Some turn out to be aggravated ingrates; it is either they have *'used', 'abused'* or *'user-dumped'* their hosts! No wonder their paths are later be-clogged with heart-rending, sympathy-evoking problems!

*Is anyone listening?*

God disfavors 'abusers', 'people-users', – and more; 'people-dumpers'!

A few years ago, a young upwardly-mobile *CEO* of a company had suddenly deftly changed the terms of contract of his employees that had affected their abilities to book holidays – and claim holiday pays. These were the exact words the Lord had sent him through me:

> *"Beware, your under-workers today, in a sudden tilt of destiny could control your great empire tomorrow – even to the denial of your set pieces!"*

It didn't take a long while before those words came true. This is because we have a precedent for every possible human scenario, in the Word of God. Remember Laban? He too had lost it all to Jacob his former worker.[16]

God clearly warns:

> *"Thou shalt not oppress an hired servant that is poor and needy ...*
>
> *At his day thou shalt give him his hire, neither shall the sun go down upon it; for he is poor and setteth his heart upon it: lest he cry against thee unto the LORD: and it be sin unto thee."*
> Deuteronomy 24:14-15

Notice the phrase: *"at his day"*, as it is very important. This literally means "the same day a worker's wage is due to be paid"; it *should* be paid!

Again, we read:

> *"Thou shalt not defraud thy neighbour, neither rob him: the wages of him that is hired shall not abide with thee all night until the morning."*
> Leviticus 19:13

Beware of *any* financial mis-appropriations; they are the *'foxes'* hugely responsible for the collapse of most personal, public or huge financial empires.

*Is God already re-defining you?*

## Defining Delay by the Six Major Reactions of Delay Sufferers

If you are still harboring any doubts about whether or not the persistent trouble on your pathway is as a result of delay, this book is intended for you! Meditatively read these few reactions of delay-sufferers, and draw realistic conclusions.

*Reaction # 1: Exhibiting a sense of Inadequacy.*
*People who have suffered delayed aspirations exhibit a sense of inadequacy.* They feel below *par*. This feeling of inadequacy encourages sufferers to begin to compare their achievements in life with their friends and colleagues. As they feel threatened, they build around themselves emotional walls and fortresses for *self*-comfort, *self*-security and *self*-preservation. If challenged, they exit for quick cover or run into their comfort zones of fortresses. They may become isolated and depressed in the process. Sufferers may become lonely, ashamed and guilty to admit it to any, the extent of the pains of missed opportunities of yester-years. They could be unreasonably touchy! They may have lost zest for accomplishment, the furtherance of and the completion of a project. They easily give in to external pressures or fleshly desires.

*Reaction # 2: Signs of Desperation.*
Apart from gross inadequacy feelings tempered with withdrawal often into the solace of self-built dilapidated 'Walls of Jericho', *prolonged delay sufferers more often than not become desperate.*

They may eventually become 'desperados'!

Their emotions and personalities could at will, swing in and out; like the dangling pendulum. They may not be stable financially, socially, emotionally and mentally; they are the type of people who rebound from one failed relationship attempt unto another without taking a moment off dating in a reflective, introspective look into their personal inadequacies and shortcomings. They easily blame others for their misfortunes. Few cases un-attended have developed bi-polar disorders and personalities. Sufferers could so soon assume the irrationality of *terminators, exterminators or eliminators!* The ten other spies had *spiced up* the ignorant bunch of emancipated children of Israel into a mob with a burning intent to execute Caleb and Joshua; the duo who appeared to have withstood their evil plans of retrogressing to Egypt.

*Reaction # 3: Rumor-mongering Signs.*
*Delay sufferers have a second nature called rumor-mongering.* Since they had lost their senses of timing and accomplishment to boisterous battles of life – and possibly mid-life crisis issues – sufferers have often been discovered to have chosen the lofty task next to idleness; that is, spreading rumors! Or gossiping! These are they whom Job warned could wage the war of *"the scourge of the tongue."*[17]

Watch your spirit lest you become spiritually *paparazzical*!

*Reaction # 4: Exhibiting Signs of Discontent due to Barrenness.* While it would be wrong to oversimplify, yet it would be found truthful to a larger extent that *people who have not been productive may exhibit strong signs of discontent.* The Bible names "a barren womb" as one of the four entities that are never easily satiable.[18] Barrenness or un-productivity may force people to become possessive – in exchange for the void they feel deep, within.

More, barrenness could often be accompanied by psychological irritable feelings for the fruitful. Barrenness or fruitlessness may make folk drift into psychosis under the slightest pressure, in their attempt to compete with or out-perform the required *status quo*. Therefore, they end up *hung on* something, for a *lean on!* Their *'lean on'* could range from joyfully volunteering to baby-sit a friend's child but ending up running away with him/her, to such uncontrollable craving for *Class A* drugs!

*Reaction # 5: Insomnia Symptoms.*
*Most delay sufferers that I have counseled suffer insomnia* – that is the inability to sleep at night. Kept awake into the *wee* hours of the morning, therefore; they often are *late morning starters* and *late night crashers!*

A thick cloud of depression looms over their heads.

If they must wake up, for instance, to go to work; insomniacs are often prone to fatigue and stress. If they are drivers, they are the likely beings prone to cause you an accident between the rush-hour traffic in October and November in the UK, when the early morning wintry sun's slanting rays slash across the windshield, directly into the driver's eyes.

Insomniacs are drained of the inner strength supplied by the heavenly joy described in *Nehemiah 8:10*.

Inevitably therefore, any who lacks inner joy would likely become a complainer, a mumbler or an ingrate! If you fitted into my description, help is available through the wisdom of God. Seek counsel. Seek help.

*Reaction # 6: Pity-party-Gathering.*
Like the ten spies in our story, *delay sufferers will certainly gather pity-parties* where coup-plots or mutinous thoughts are likely to be hatched.

Be careful to not honor their invitation.

*Delay Exposé*

# The 'Me-Me' Chart

| Hues and Cries | Root Cause(s) | Behavioral Reflection |
| --- | --- | --- |
| "Oh, Poor Me!" | Poverty. Wasted opportunities. Idleness. Slothfulness. | Regretful. Self-pity. Confusion. Envy. *Laisser-faire.* Rumor/Gossip mongering! |
| "Help me ..." | No self worth. Lazy. Opportunist. Lack of insight, intuition and divine ideas. Fear of failure! Insecurities of various types. | Overwhelmed Manipulative Indifferent to others' plights! |
| *Suicidal thoughts, Self harm*! | Built up emotional distress! Deep hurts/resentment. The spirit of depression/heaviness. | Psychotic. Suicidal. Manipulative. Lying-spirited. |
| "Marry me, I need you." | Insecurity. *Eros* passion *per se.* Thoughts about not losing the physical looks or the material gains in a person targeted as an intended victim of emotional abuse. | Lustful. Witchcraft manipulative tendencies. Sensual. *Desperado!* |
| *Uncontrollable sobs* | Deep soul anguish and pain. True remorse and penitence. Unpleasant memory flashbacks. | Reflective of true love lost. Remorseful of a sinful act. Godly-sorrowful and prayerful. Could be bitter, revengeful or forgiving which leads to restoration. |

*Destroying the Power of Delay*

| | | |
|---|---|---|
| "Release me! Let me out!" | Un-submissiveness! Abuse. Oppression. Lawlessness. | Rebellious. Prodigal. Factional! |
| "Never me ... Not my fault." | Guilt feelings denied. Emotionally damaged. Wearing numerous scars! | Apathetic. Blame-shifting and hardened. Unstable. Unreliable. Cheater. Loose and shamelessly immoral. Irresponsible. Blameful. |
| "Please, reason with me!" | Repentant. Lack of integrity. Incredulity. Fear of rejection! | Argumentative. Jittery Asks for a second chance. Peacemaking. |
| "Me ... me; I ... I ... I" | Pride! Lust for power and control. Ego. Selfishness. Greed! | *'Luciferic.'* Loud and noisy. Domineering. Greedy. Egoistic. |

Having unraveled the mysteries surrounding delay by unraveling and exposing its bulb-foliage wraps, my hope is that you would be able to seek help where needed. This chapter would be grossly incomplete without my sharing about *the* winning reaction over any type of delay: it is the reaction of a caged eagle!

## *The Reaction of a caged Eagle*

A bald eagle in captivity; restrained, pensive, mournful, yet thoughtful. It's head bent; eyes set in hollowed, far looks. A soaring *"freedom bird"*, there is never a higher punishment that could be meted out to the bald eagle than restrict it. Its long feathers droop and soon begin to quilt. Its weight plummets considerably since it has begun to refuse food; these are a few of his natural reactions to *this* alien circumstance, its captivity! It looks ever weaker as the day passes; yet stronger in the hope of *spirit de corps* of eagles!

*Does this describe you – or someone you know?*

Hope has not *really* become hope if it has not rejoiced *against* hopelessness and helplessness. This bird is broken, humbled and sober. It has surrendered its fate to its Maker alone.

In this inactive state, an outstanding character of the eagle is worthy of a re-call: the lone-bird watches the Sun's oblong path from sunrise to sunset, entirely focused in silent, humble conversations with the Creator Who alone can make the sun rise again after a previous setting.

We understand that God looks down from the height of His sanctuary and beholds the Earth. We also know that the Almighty hears the groaning of the prisoner; to loose those that are appointed to death.[19]

In the meanwhile, this restricted strange creature is undergoing a strict reformation. This reformative work is essential; it would put in it the required mental and bodily shapes required for the inevitable launch to the next level.

When the Judge of all, in His time, eventfully releases this *reformed eagle* that had been long held captive, all of creature should be prepared to watch one of God's greatest magnificent beauties on display, soaring into its destiny.

Listen, eagles never are shy to mount up and soar into great altitudes no matter the adversity they have encountered; neither should you!

## Chapter 4

# 22 Major Causes of Delay

*"This is the ruling law in the spirit-realm, whoever talks faith, gets fit!"*
   *- Sammy Joseph*

Thus far in this book, I have hinted on the fact that life is continuous – though very short. I have also carefully mapped out destiny detour routes which you must avoid in order to arrive at *your* Canaan! *Delay-Exposé* has intrinsically delved into – and exposed – the elemental factors of *delay*.

In this chapter, I shall discuss *delay's* major causes.

From the selected portions of our text, we read, thus:

> *"And they returned from searching the land after forty days.*
> 
> *And they went and came to Moses, and to Aaron, and to all the congregation of the children of Israel, unto the wilderness of Paran, to Kadesh; and brought back word unto them, and unto all the congregation, and showed them the fruit of the land.*

*And they told him, and said, We came unto the land whither thou sentest us, and surely it floweth with milk and honey; and this is the fruit of it.*

*Nevertheless the people be strong that dwell in the land, and the cities are walled, and very great: and moreover we saw the children of Anak there.*

*And Caleb stilled the people before Moses, and said, Let us go up at once, and possess it; for we are well able to overcome it.*

*But the men that went up with him said, We be not able to go up against the people; for they are stronger than we.*

*And they brought up an evil report of the land which they had searched unto the children of Israel, saying, The land, through which we have gone to search it, is a land that eateth up the inhabitants thereof; and all the people that we saw in it are men of a great stature.*

*And there we saw the giants, the sons of Anak, which come of the giants: and we were in our own sight as grasshoppers, and so we were in their sight.*

*And all the congregation lifted up their voice, and cried; and the people wept that night.*

*And all the children of Israel murmured against Moses and against Aaron: and the whole congregation said unto them, Would God that we had died in the land of Egypt! or would God we had died in this wilderness!*

*And wherefore hath the LORD brought us unto this land,*

*to fall by the sword, that our wives and our children should be a prey? Were it not better for us to return into Egypt?*

*And they said one to another, Let us make a captain, and let us return into Egypt."*
Numbers 13:25-28; 30-33; 14:1-4

From the above portion of Scriptures, the major causes of *delay* include:

1.) *Being Intimidated by Seemingly formidable Physical Barriers:*

> *"… the cities are walled, and very great."*
> Verse 28

While these *men of sight* had submitted their destinies to fear, the much thicker and more formidable walls of Jericho would sink at the command of Joshua, *a man of faith*, in latter times. You ought not to be intimidated by the imposing barriers you may encounter *en route* Canaan!

2.) *Being Intimidated by the Towering Presence of Giants:*

> *"... and moreover we saw the children of Anak there."*
> Verse 28

The reality is that God has giants positioned, milepost to milepost on the race-tracks for excellence and the crown of life!

You should be surprised at what God calls these whom you refer to as giants; says He: *"they are bread for us."*[1] In other words, giants – life's seemingly insurmountable troubles – are *intended* nourishment sources to your spirit-man. Once you conquer one, your *inner man* is re-energized with stamina to maul another!

Testimonials to the magnanimous or the miraculous acts of God energize us collectively, in our spiritual journeys. Testimonies are birthed from giants slain! Having once conquered a lion and a bear, David had precious, vivid memories of encounters of God's deliverances to recall and draw from in order to be infused with inner strength, with which he ultimately triumphed over Goliath! When you cower back at the towering sight of a giant, however, you will potentially miss a worthy portion of nutritious ration apportioned by Heaven.

But one thing is certain: the earlier you encountered and conquered your giant; the better equipped you will become in possessing your Canaan in good time.

3.) *Possessing Inferiority Complex; the Defeatist Spirit:*

> "... and we were in our own sight as grasshoppers, and so we were in their sight."
>
> Verse 33

You must be bold, brave and creative. God has *not* gifted you with the spirit that feels either grossly incomplete or slightly inadequate; the grasshopper mentality! Like it or not, I am surrounded with an aura of a superior mind-frame, higher than the giants I encounter. Dwelling in the assurance of God's presence has enabled me in my call to do the in-conceivable to the natural mind.

No one will follow a *wimp*; leaders are called to be bold and brave – even in the wake of an adversity. Potential suitors seeking life-partners are quick to *smell* insecure people like white-sharks do blood traces in the ocean. No employer will offer a job to a person who already looks defeated and unsure of themselves. Securing that job, therefore, certainly is not based upon great brains only; personal deferment and comportment are of a significant importance. Appear *chic*, confident of who you are – and whose, you are! Wear a sunny, cheerful disposition. *"Cast not away therefore your confidence, which hath a great recompense of reward"* (Hebrews 10:35).

4.) *Negative Verbal Confessions:*

> *"We be not able to go up ... for they are stronger than we."*
> Verse 31

Negative verbal confessions are self-inflicted curses.

In the *foundational classes* of English education, teachers taught: *"Words and Opposite."* Now, if the spies that were sent to spy Canaan confessed that they *be not able to go up,* they surely would, without question, *be able to come down.* If they confirmed the giants to be stronger, it was mandatory they would be weaker!

Throughout scriptures, God warns us to speak *only* positive words of faith even though we may be besieged by negative scenery! This is not *lie-telling*; rather, it is *like-telling* with God!

This is the ruling edict in the spirit-realm: whoever talks faith gets fit!

5.) *Murmuring, Grumbling or Complaining:*

> *"Neither murmur ye, as some of them also murmured and were destroyed of the destroyer."*
> 1 Corinthians 10:10

The evil habits of murmuring or grumbling are as rottenness in the bones. Either is an indication of the presence of the *"piggy spirit."*

Of sins in the 'top-ten' chart committed by the Israelites, *murmuring* occupied an early, prominent slot – third in ranking after idolatry in the first and adultery/fornication in the second, respectively! Now you understand why God dis-inherited close to three million people of the promise of possessing Canaan – but their offspring who eventually obtained the promise had also suffered *delay* by a generation!

Be warned: murmuring, grumbling and complaining could delay you close to forty years!

*6.) Rumor-mongering:*
Rumors are *not* wholesome, untrue reports! Certainly, there couldn't be anything more diabolical in motive than mixing just a little lie with the whole chunk of truth – which rumors, infact, are. The motive of rumor mongering is to mislead a cause; cause confusion, a bias – and/possibly a revolt. I shall deploy the tool of a *question and answer* session to further buttress my assertion about rumor-mongering.

- *Was Canaan a fertile land flowing with milk and honey?*

*Yes!* The spies had brought with them one cluster of grapes cut from Eshcol borne by two heavy men *(verse 23)*.

- *Were there giants, sons of Anak, actually on site in Canaan?*

*Yes, very much so – and by all means!* The Bible confirms the presence of fierce-looking giants *(verse 32)*.

- *Did the spies accomplish a comprehensive espionage mission?*

*Again, the answer is in the affirmative: Yes!* The spies did accomplish a comprehensive espionage mission, as evidently included in the *logistics feedback* they submitted to Moses *(verse 29).*

7.) *Exaggeration:*
The first exaggeration the spies made was that of the giants' sizes:

> *"... and we were in our own sight as grasshoppers, and so we were in their sight."*
> Verse 33

Our focal questions are: *"Did the twelve spies really measure themselves side by side the giants - and did they take an opinion poll of the giants' perception of them?"*

I very much doubt the possibilities of those suppositions, above, having occurred.

Their second exaggerated claim was that the land was *"a land that eateth up the inhabitants thereof."*[2] If this had been true, *"Why hadn't the frequent earthquake and tremor occurrences swallowed up the very giant population?"*

The third exaggerated claim was most confusing; the disgruntled, mutinous spies had rumored that Canaan had been fortified by a great wall![3]

I dare ask: *"Was Canaan truly fortified by a great wall?"*

*Strong's New Exhaustive Concordance* of the Bible lists lands or landsites that were walled in those times; nowhere did Dr. Strong or other Bible commentators suggest Canaan being greatly fortified as the ten evil spies had unjustly exaggerated!

Strong's list of fortified locations included *the notable walls of Jericho; the walls of:* Betshan (1 Samuel 31:10); Thebez (2 Samuel 11:21); the city of David (2 Samuel 18:24); Abel of Bethmaachah (2 Samuel 20:15); Jezreel (1 Kings 21:23); the wall of Jerusalem (2 Kings 3:1); Hazor, Megiddo and Gezer (1 Kings 9:15). Other walls mentioned include those of Gath, Jabneh and Ashdod of the Philistines (2 Chronicles 26:6).

Continuing, we read of walls *of Ophel (2 Chronicles 27:3); the Pool of Siloa (Nehemiah 3:15); walls of Babylon (Jeremiah 51:12); Tyrus (Ezekiel 26:4); Damascus (Jeremiah 49:27); wall of the Temple (Ezekiel 41:20); Gaza (Amos 1:7); Rabbah (Amos 1:14); No (Nahum 3:8)* and *Damascus (Acts 9:25).* The last reference to the city with walls is the *Heavenly City (Revelations 21:12-14).*

God calls rumors and exaggerated claims, evil reports.[4]

### 8.) Maintaining Wrong Associations:
Maintaining and servicing wrong destructive link(s) will threaten to jettison the destiny of the wrongly associated. *If you have parted ways with an old flame – and they are now engaged to be married or legally married, why would you still be exchanging texts, tweets, e-mails or phone calls requesting for a 'meet up', or a day out?*

I shall examine these doomed association types in greater detail in latter part of the book, but here; we see Joshua and Caleb who possessed *"another spirit"* un-avoidably mismatched with the wrong company of majority spies. The mismatch percentage ratio was an abhorrent 17%:83%. This translates one good man being surrounded by five over-powering evil men.

God did not anymore reserve the resolve to absolve Caleb and Joshua from the thirty-eight year scourge of wandering in the desert than they both did; though, He would in His mercy, preserve the duo to enter and inherit Canaan.

9.) *Mingling with Mutiny Groups:*

*How would you recognize a mutinous group?*

Firstly, *a mutinous group usually originates from within a church, an organization or a family.*

Secondly, *mutinous groups are headed by a faction leader* who himself/herself had been a part of and possessed the insider's knowledge of the leadership structure of an establishment.

Thirdly, *mutinies dissent on non-essential, trivial issues, thus making mountains out of molehills.*

Fourthly, *a mutinous spirit locks in on breaking away and creating schisms in the Body rather than reconciliation.*

Fifthly, *mutiny always aims at the set-person or the visioner with an urgent mandate for his/her replacement!*[5]

Please do not *side up* with the rebellious party. God has always disinherited mutineers. Do *not* hatch a plot against your local shepherd because of his righteous stance on issues regarding immorality. Do not disinherit *yourself* from entering in – and possessing *your* Canaan.

10.) *'Laying Hands' on God's Anointed Servant:*

> *"But all the congregation bade stone them with stones..."*
> Numbers 14:10

Familiarity breeds contempt. There are many ways folk could lay hands on the anointed servant of God: attack through the *sword of the mouth;* an untamed tongue, or a writer's pen; belittling looks or gestures, rumor-mongering and the like.

When you scheme any of these means of attack against your intended victim, depending directly proportionally to the richness and depth of anointing they carry, you automatically release the curse of delay, destruction and death upon your destiny.

Spouses of God's servants – in particular – need to fully support and be involved with their married partners in fulfilling their ministries lest they become tempted with insecure feelings, jealousy, irritation or fall for the deception of *the feelings of neglect*!

Some aggravated spouses have given the devil a foothold in this particular area – and have slid into heavy depression – with a heinous determination to either physically assault, maim – or indeed, murder their minister spouses!

No matter what your relationship with a servant of God is, resist getting too familiar with them.

The glory of the Lord showed up and evoked hot wrath upon the dissenters: *"Even those men that did bring up the evil report upon the land, died by the plague before the LORD. But Joshua the son of Nun, and Caleb the son of Jephunneh, which were of the men that went to search the land lived still."*[6]
Hasn't God advised: *"Touch not mine anointed, and do my prophets no harm"*[7]?

11.) *Sympathy-seeking/Self-pity:*

> *"And all the congregation lifted up their voice and cried; and the people wept that night."*
> 
> Numbers 14:1

The ten mutiny chiefs had bewitched the people, their emotions be-swayed.

Self-pity is self destructive enough. Sympathy-seeking however destroys both the seeker and the giver(s).

Do *not* deliberately seek others' sympathy; neither encourage *pitty-patters* to pitch tents adjacent to yours: they would surely inflate your emotions and swing you onto destructive paths.

Sympathy seekers are lonely and frustrated enough – thus they earnestly scout for new recruits, *"wandering about from house to house (or phone number to number); and not only idle, but tattlers and busybodies, speaking things which they ought not"*, as Apostle Paul rendered their description in 1 Timothy 5:13; emphasis in bracket, mine.

Simply refuse to mortgage your destiny!

*12.) Fear of the Unknown in Relocating, Changing Lifestyles or Engaging New Methods and Innovations:*
Having compassed Mount Seir many days, it was a natural thought to the complacent throng of people to conceive that God would let them settle in the adjoining patches of land surrounding the mountain!

*Who wants to go fight killer giants in Canaan, anyway?*

Suddenly, contrary to their expectations, God spoke to Moses: *"You have compassed this mountain long enough: turn you northward."*[8]

Either the fear or euphoric thrill of the unknown has ruined the prospects of – or worked to the advantage of –

intelligent scientific discoveries and formidable new frontier settlers! Life's territories for the taking are intrinsically marked:

> "Not for the Fearful nor the Doubtful!"

Gaining advantage through life's adventures will require you to make sound choices. Personally, one more choice I have decided: to gainfully exploit – with the view to *take and master* at least, a new *territory of life*, each year!

13.) *The Use of Human Shields as Instruments to Perpetrate Rebellion:*

> "And wherefore hath the LORD brought us unto this land, to fall by the sword, that our wives and our children should be a prey? were it not better for us to return into Egypt?"
> Numbers 14:3

*Human shields* are mainly deployed at warfronts. They are an arraignment of innocent, defenseless humans, strategically placed at outlawed arenas so as to avert a lawful assault on such places. Saddam Hussein's pockets of resistant *Elite Guards* during *Operation Desert Storm* used hundreds of innocent children as human shields at hospitals packed full with offensive military arsenals. He thought he was buying time. You and I know he wasn't! These Canaan-bound Israelites also were *buying* time. They had grown complacent. *"Life was manageable enough,"* they had mused.

*"Why venture out facing the risk of fighting the giants when our wives and children would be susceptible to the Anakims' reprisal attacks? Hey, why loose our posterity because of Canaan?"*

The *fathers* in the Wilderness *used* their loved ones as potential *human shields* against the backdrop of their personal unwillingness to obey God advancing against the giants and possessing Canaan.

*Are you also constructing human-shield excuses to delay obeying God?*

Other ways of employing the use of *human shields* to avoid the substance of matter *in situ* include:

*i.) Parental dictates to a child, of a life career:*
This practice is most rampant with parents who, themselves, are professionally trained; for instance, medical doctors, solicitors, engineers, accountants *(et cetera)*; they who envision their children stepping into their shoes. Good as their intentions may seem, it has an inherent deft touch of parental manipulative tendencies! Otherwise, parents who had failed in their original pursuits in life may possess strong wishes to make it good on their children to live out the vision they themselves had failed to envision. These parents may find themselves applying manipulative pressures on the next generation to live out their failed dreams.

ii.) *An ungodly attachment to your son/daughter – thus not granting them the spiritual release for marriage when they are ripe and of marriageable age:*
Do you prefer your child(ren) to still serve as your companion in old age; thus you contrive of all possible means to manipulate and *use* them as a protective shield against loneliness in your advancing years?

Do you probably intend the most prominent of your children to be hand-picked and *used* as suitable financial guarantors/sureties in your old age?

*If your answers to either or both questions above are in the affirmative, then, you are of such parents who hold their children responsible as tributes to re-pay your financial mistakes; make good, your misfortunes or recoup the precious mid-life time you spent alone with them after your divorce!*

You may not even realize it; but your actions have been instigated by the insinuation of the *'Pharaohic spirit.'*

You're almost a dead meat!

*Why did I say this?*

My affirmation, above, is prevalent upon the truth that whenever the *'spirit of Pharaoh'* has been confronted and dislodged in the name of the Lord of Hosts – and his enslaving grip broken; sudden physical death has always been the repercussion on the possessor of such menial spirit! *"Let my people go,"* saith the Lord.[9]

*iii.) Not releasing your child/ward to pursue the call of God upon their lives:*
If it is a clarion call of God to your child, ward or any, under your scope of influence and authority to pursue a life of service in the christian ministry, please do *not* restrain or persecute them. Rather, encourage them with godly wisdom on how to fulfill such call! Children are *not* personal items of belonging of either parents or custodians; children *"are an heritage of the Lord."*[10]

*iv.) Jealous parents or authority figures:*
Parents, bosses and authority figures that are jealous of the series of opportunities portrayed before their children, employees and subjects shall certainly turn around to *'use'* those committed to them purely for financial gains.

*v.) Upbraiding children:*
Angry parents who upbraid their children; that is, render an unhealthy account of gifts given to, sacrifices made for or costs incurred in training those children in their moments of displeasure – or at any other times will provoke such children to wrath.[11]

*vi.) Using children as 'human missiles':*
Not only could children be used as *'human shields'*, they could also be used, potentially, as *'missiles'* and/weapons of warfare. For instance, when a discordant parent incenses or instructs a child to behave in certain unruly and unethical ways as a launchpad of a pre-meditated, pre-calculated attack against the other parent; both the parent and the child(ren) in question would potentially carry the curse of God![12]

## *Other Possible Causes of Delay*

• *Presumptuous Obedience:*
Proposing "advancement" when God restrains; or delaying when God motions "advancement" would ultimately lead to a catastrophe. That was exactly what befell the Israelites:

> *"But they presumed to go up into the hill top: nevertheless the ark of the covenant of the LORD, and Moses, departed not out of the camp.*
>
> *Then the Amalekites came down, and the Canaanites which dwelt in that hill, and smote them, and discomfited them, even unto Hormah."*
>
> Numbers 14:44-45

It was the same *error of presumption* that had killed Uzzah when he had steadied the Ark of the Covenant by his *'supportive'* touch.[13]

- *Possessing an Accursed thing:*

Anytime anyone had taken custody of that which was not legally, customarily or morally theirs, *the* curse had been put into effect. Naaman's leprosy would eternally cling unto Gehazi and his lineage for a handful of changeover garments. Achan's entire household would perish alongside him for a bar of gold not worth more than $500 USD.[14] Rachel, Jacob's wife would be brought to her grave, earlier than God had ordained, for the sake of mere images – or title deeds – of her father Laban's, she had stolen from him.[15]

If you possess any document, title deed, conveyance papers *et cetera* – which have been stolen, pilfered or purloined; the only escape route away from God's wrath is to repent and change the thought process that has led you this far. Then, you will restore the ill-possessed goods and title deeds.[16]

*16.) Sisera's Errors:*

Doomsday King Sisera had been shooting himself in the foot; little wonder his drastic collapse! Learn from his errors as recounted in Judges 4:17-21.

*Sisera's Error # 1:*
*Do not stay with your friend's spouse in the absence of your friend* regardless of the level of relationship you may profess to maintain. Do *not* give room for error of judgment: affairs *do* necessarily begin with emotional attachments – but do *not* get fulfilled, necessarily, in carnal knowledge of each other![17]

*Sisera's Error # 2:*
*Whenever you are unduly pampered with extravagant hospitality; beware!* Trouble probably looms behind your host's motive for the exceptional treatment received. Sisera had asked for *"a little water to drink"*, but Jael had opened for him *"a bottle of milk"* – yet the bloke was un-assuming and un-suspicious of a foul intent.[18]

Sisera's *Error # 3:*
*Requesting others to tell a 'cover up' lie is too sure a tell-tale sign of a blurry ending.* Jael's 'womanly conscience' was quickly sensitized; Jabin, earmarked for destruction!

While we learn from Jabin's errors, please spare me a moment to make a comment! On most campuses of higher learning in Africa, many a *sheepish*, unwary, simple-minded girl had been invited out by a girl-friend to an un-named third friend's party, unaware of their real intent. They had both slept over. The night had turned into day. Her understanding had just awakened; the previous night's invitation had been to her peril: she had been plied with a strong drink and had been grossly abused. The attack had been perpetrated by a long-pending, secret admirer-boy she had eventually danced with! She was too ashamed to tell anyone; her best-friend had betrayed her trust for *a mint*!

Other times though, a boy could have acted the *'pimp'* for a sugar-daddy with a burning mandate to produce him a virgin girl!

*17.) Being Malicious or Envious of Those Fruitful:*
God would become man! To begin with, He ended Elizabeth's prolonged reproach of barrenness; she became pregnant. Half year later, Angel Gabriel appeared to Mary

informing her of Heaven's intent. The Virgin girl acted so outstandingly: she made a decision – and followed it through – to go rejoice with her pregnant cousin, Elizabeth; *with haste!*

> *"And Mary arose in those days, and went into the hill country with haste, into a city of Juda ..."*
> Luke 1:39

Did you notice that it was while Virgin Mary was in the act of rejoicing with Elizabeth, that the *Heavenly IVF transplant* that would change the course of the destiny of the universe was completed in her womb?[19]

Cousin Elizabeth perceived in the spirit, the moment of conception of the Holy Seed inside of Mary. She cried out aloud:

> *"Blessed art thou among women, and blessed is the fruit of thy womb."*
> Luke 1:38-42

Whenever the Heavens herald the season of somebody's fruitfulness and you go rejoice with them, your fruitfulness should soon be broadcast.

*18.) Un-utilized Opportunities:*
Indecision of the lover in Solomon's love-poems to open the door of her heart to her beloved at the opportuned time ensured her loss of same when she came to her right mind. But he was nowhere to be found. Soul-anguish and turmoil enraged within her; she went searching for him – and encountered many a peril, all to no avail.[20]

Ladies who do *not* know when to stop playing "hard-to-get" have always arrived at the same conclusion: *"Better make hay whilst the sun shines!"*

Love-sickness apart, psychologists and psycho-analysts have also reasoned that opportunities missed or un-utilized restrain and weaken the mind's zest to pursing other equally likely opportunities!

19.) *Disorientation about Delay/Adopting the Wrong Mental Approach tackling Delay:*
Dr. Robert Schuller of *Chrystal Cathedral*, Garden Grove, California, made famous the quote: *"Delay is No Denial."* And yes; while delay is never a denial, yet, our disorientation or mis-conceptualization about tackling delay will result in utter frustration!

Take for instance, someone expecting an "open door" would necessarily be mandated to await the opening, by God, of such a door! But they must *not* wait doing nothing. You see, the pursuance of *nothing* while awaiting *something* is averse to right scripture-thinking! (I have in great details addressed this particular topic in my book: GIDEON: *Releasing the Potentials Within You*, published *by Pulse Publishing House, revised edition 2011, Chapters 3 & 4*).

20.) *Lack of Understanding and Depth in things of the Spirit:*

*"Deep calleth unto deep at the noise of thy waterspouts ..."*
Psalms 42:7

God's universe is governed by God's laws. If any man would propel himself into the *mechanics* of God's operations, undeniable results usually follow. Take for instance, a person who pays their wholesome tithe – that is 10% of their incomes, what such is affirming is their declaration to God, the angels, the devil and his demons in all the five existential realms of life: *"I am a covenant-keeper!"* The devil and his demons decode the message: *"Get lost, Satan, from me – and all mine! I am covered by the deeds of the Blood-covenant."*

However, if they refuse to honor God with their firstfruits and tithes, they will live a mandatory *tight* lifestyle!

Let me offer you another example where possessing the spirit of understanding is essential.

If your church's building project is in an uncompleted state whilst you further the construction of your *"ceiled houses"*, furthering it unto completion, God's Spirit will necessarily put you at unrest. By this disenfranchised posture of yours, you have signed God a permit to allow the devourer to automatically assign your pocket with various holes of differing sizes. These are the *holes* in your pocket which drain your finances, earnings, wages, efforts and *real* potentials![21] Certain unforeseen incidents, illnesses, accidents, and disappointments of various sorts suddenly occur. You must understand, now, why these evils are happening. Stop and negotiate a U-turn maneuver, in repentance.

And talking of special offerings, Israel had at least eight major types of special offerings; namely: *sin offering, freewill offering, heave offering, burnt offering, meat offering, wave offering, drink offering and peace offering.*

Just shortly after he ascended the throne of Israel, Solomon offered an outlandish *peace offering* unto the LORD! The consequence was that his land had peace – in fact, an abundance of peace, the whole of his tenure! Solomon didn't need to attend a single war. Rather, he was a wise king who compensated for what he didn't possess with what he did understand about the ways of God's workings!

Wouldn't it be proper to affirm therefore, that a special *peace offering* offered unto the LORD *of Hosts* should ensure the total destruction of the delay jinx that has plagued your life?

*21.) Harboring an Un-confessed, Un-repented Secret Sin:*
An un-confessed secret sin definitely would hinder your ability to *possess* your destiny! If you enjoy committing secret sins, you must endure postponing entering into your land of rest.

*What is a secret sin?*

A secret sin is a sin none else knows you commit, apart from you and God alone.

Listen, it is a great transgression for a spouse to deny the other, *the rightful matrimonial rite of passage* for any reason whatever – apart from a jointly agreed period of abstinence purely for the purposes of prayer and fasting alone. If you deny your spouse matrimonial rites of passage – that is, sex in marriage, you run two obvious risks: driving them into the arms of a strange lover; and/or, inevitably inviting a *succubus* or an *incubus* to mate with them. Either way, they *should* surely be defiled – and so would you too![22]

*22.) Unforgiveness:*
Possessing either an unforgiving spirit that wishes evil upon another – or a rejoiceful spirit that laughs at others' misfortunes or calamities – certainly will ensnare your destiny.

> *"Whoso mocketh the poor reproacheth his Maker: and he that is glad at calamities shall not be unpunished."*
>
> Proverbs 17:5

Harboring feelings of indifference and apathy towards even an enemy – or someone who had hurt or offended you – in their day of distress is offensive to God. A rightful punishment was meted out to *carnal* Esau for his un-apathetic wicked stance against Israel:

> *"But thou shouldest not have looked on the day of thy brother Jacob in the day that he became a stranger; neither shouldest thou have rejoiced over the children of Judah in the day of their destruction; neither shouldest thou have spoken proudly in the day of distress.*
>
> *Thou shouldest not have entered into the gate of my people in the day of their calamity; yea, thou shouldest not have looked on their affliction in the day of their calamity, nor have laid hands on their substance in the day of their calamity.*
>
> *Neither shouldest thou have stood in the crossway, to cut off those of his that did escape; neither shouldest thou have delivered up those of his that did remain in the day of distress."*
>
> Obadiah 12-14

May you receive the awesomeness of God's power that will be released as you put into practice these teachings. When you do, delay should never again be able to pitch tents on your destiny-journey's mileposts.

# Chapter 5

# Deliverance from Inextricable Covenant Relationships

*"The reputation of a thousand years may be determined by the conduct of one hour."*
                                            - A Japanese proverb

The book of first Samuel, the twenty-fifth chapter opens with the death of Prophet Samuel and the overwhelming national mourning held in his honor by all Israel - including in particular, David his protégé. David knew of his inestimable loss. He knew the treasured physical and spiritual values Prophet Samuel had offered him. Yet, all these had suddenly *'vaporized'*; so David departed for a more secluded place, in the desert of Paran to mourn Samuel's death in a state of utter brokenness of heart.

Despite his huge loss, though, there was yet an uncommunicated issue pressing very hard on his heart, against his rib-cage! This is the second part of the story told in this same chapter.

## Mid Life Crises in Men

There is no such term as "mid-life crisis" in the Bible; nevertheless it existed even in biblical times, for both sexes! However, I am limiting myself to this time of life in the male – for reasons, solely pertinent to our study!

*Mid life crises* in men may arrive at different times and seasons of their lives. For some, they suddenly discover the hairs at the crown of their heads are thinning out; for others, it's a sudden discovery of a need for a forward-adjustment of the belt buckle-hole. A top executive may find himself suddenly made redundant; he would have to re-strategize.

Some men may wrongly react to the adversity of this period of time of their lives by growing distasteful of the enriching vital intimacy that should have deepened between themselves and their wives. For some reasons, they begin to get tempted to withdraw inwards – but ironically start to nurse thoughts of and flourish in the desire for a younger woman, if quick care is not taken.

For David, a string of events led to the different crises in his life: it had all stemmed from his slaughter of the giant, Goliath, at age fourteen. Because of king Saul's insecurity; jealousy of and outrage at the young man, David – even though destined to ascend upon the throne of Israel – would hide in caves and skip around the bare, rugged terrains of the wilderness, escaping from the annihilative threats of Saul for more than two decades!

In this fugitive state of existence, coupled with anxiety, anger, loneliness, frustration – and a concocted, less-than-stable-state-of-mind, David would encounter the unimaginable duo of Mr. and Mrs. Nabal!

Hear me well: one quick lesson that needs be safely tucked away at the back of your mind ought to be your mindfulness to *not* add in any additional way(s) to the torture of *the broken*. These are people already undergoing a humiliation, bereavement, defeat, delay or loss; thus broken by life's unpredictable circumstances. Flaunt this rule and you would have violated one of God's universe's finest rules: *the right to privacy, the protection of human sense of dignity and the law of harmonious co-existence.*

My counter-advice Sir Nabal would exactly heed!

Let's meet Nabal – and his wife, Abigail!

## *Inextricable Relationship #1: Nabal and Abigail Marriage Types*

> *"And there was a man in Maon, whose possessions were in Carmel; and the man was very great, and he had three thousand sheep, and a thousand goats: and he was shearing his sheep in Carmel.*
>
> *Now the name of the man was Nabal; and the name of his wife Abigail: and she was a woman of good understanding, and of a beautiful countenance; but the man was churlish and evil in his doings; and he was of the house of Caleb."*
>
> 1 Samuel 25:2-3

## *Digging Deeper*

Nabal's name meant *"a fool"*; Abigail's, *"the joy of a father."* Now, Nabal was a direct descendant of Caleb – the same Caleb and Joshua team. Infact, Nabal had inherited Caleb's Estates of Maon and Carmel situated near Hebron; these were his main source of wealth.[1] It was easier to multiply sheep, oxen and goats once the issue of the meadows had been established for all time. Sir Nabal possessed gigantic business acumen though he was a midget in godly virtues and understanding.

Hence, the question begging for an answer is this: *"Who really is rich? Is it he who is:*

- *rich in goods and not God;*

- *rich in God and not goods;*

- *rich in goods and gods, or;*

- *rich in God and goods?"*

I believe firmly you have rightly chosen the correct answer![2]

Not only was Nabal *poor* toward God, he was of *poor* manners. The Bible describes him as *"churlish."* That translates he was *"a grunt, like a pig."* He was surly, snappish and always snarling like a dog. More, he was proud, loud and rude. Summarily, the Bible says Nabal *"was rough and evil in his doings."*[3]

As I am yet to meet any who was bitter on the inside and had escaped the harrowing furrows of facial wrinkles,

Nabal; I presume, must have been a very ugly man indeed! *Ugly but rich.* This was the man Abigail was inextricably joined unto, in an everlasting wedlock.

Quite to the contrary, Abigail was a ravishing *beaut!* She was a woman *"of a beautiful countenance."*[4] I have attended many a wedding ceremony and have heard people's comments of the like: *"How did she manage to win the guy's heart?"* Or *"What on earth did she find attractive in him?"*

Physical beauty apart, Abigail possessed inner beauties. This is she whom the Bible commends searchful, eligible bachelor-suitors to acutely target; an inner beauty, bedecked in an ornament of a meek and quiet spirit, which in the sight of God is of an inestimable price.[5]

Not only was Abigail physically and spiritually attractive, the Bible says that *"She was a woman of good understanding."*[6]

*When one has understanding, what does this mean?*

To have *understanding* is to have the ability to know *"how to"* successfully approach the diverse, wide-ranging issues of life. You cannot extricate *'understanding'* away from a full possession first, of the Holy Spirit of God and the Word of God. The *"spirit of understanding"* is one of the inseparable seven-fold spirits of the LORD found in Isaiah 11:2:

> *"And the spirit of the LORD shall rest upon him, the spirit of wisdom and understanding, the spirit of counsel and might, the spirit of knowledge and of the fear of the LORD."*

Now, if *knowledge* concerns *knowing* and *wisdom* pertains to *doing* what is known; then an *understanding mind* would imply a mind that is assured of the certainty of the outcome of knowledge applied to solve a problem. *An understanding mind comes with the unshakeable conviction that God will remain faithful to His word to bring it to come to pass, whatever He had declared to execute.*

Now, I know the next question agitating your mind: *"If Abigail knew the Lord, and was a woman of understanding; why did she marry a fool – as glaring a fool, as Nabal?"*

Well, the most plausible reasons why Abigail *had* married Nabal might have included – but certainly not restricted to – the following:

• Abigail had at the time of her wedding not been as *spiritually matured* as she'd later become in latter years;

• She had been *deluded by the endearing effects of Nabal's riches* during courtship;

• Poor sister Abigail had been *forcefully married* to Nabal by a father who had an eye on Nabal's vast riches. (Worse could it have been if the marriage deal had been secured by a *Jezebelitish* mother who had been hell-bent on ensuring her futuristic financial security against old age at the sacrifice of her daughter's soul); or,

• Abigail had *deliberately compromised and laid aside the Spirit's restraints* in courtship/engagement, blinded by love!

Reassuringly, *any* of the conditions above could have been the case then, as it could possibly be, today!

But because the Bible remains silent on reasons why Abigail had agreed to marry Nabal, no one may be able to accurately offer any particular clues! What I can re-assure you of is the Lord's unwavering faithfulness as the Bishop and Shepherd of our souls – even in the times of deep sorrow and mis-choices!

His gentle Spirit would have warned such *"Abigails"* of the dire consequences their recklessness would earn them, if they willfully proceeded to marry such *"Nabals"*.

Quite unfortunately, though, Abigail eventually legally became Mrs. Abigail Nabal. In no sooner time, she probably would begin to grow tired and weary of such a mismatched union of drain and pain!

Nabal on the other was a brute; he could not have cared more!

## *Wisdom Handling Situations Involving Inextricable Relationships*

*Do you still remember the story of the twelve spies sent to espy Canaan?*

Nabal's great fore-uncle Caleb was one – of the group of two – who had found himself *hammed in as tuna in a sandwich* of ten other incorrigible colleagues. Joseph and Moses amidst their rivaling siblings were the only other preceding examples in the whole of scriptures, who had been wrongly and inextricably mismatched in relationships.

One thing was certain: once linked to that faith-less generation, God would not expunge Caleb's and Joshua's names from the list of wanderers that would roam the desert in the forty year-sentence of destiny detour that had wasted close to three million doubtful souls. Joseph would suffer a thirteen year delay; Moses, banished by death, from the precincts of Canaan!

Like Abigail, David would wed Michal under the most bizarre of circumstances. Michal had fallen in love with David's charms and qualities. That only worsened matters: being of a relatively humble background, David wasn't up to the beat of becoming the king's son-in-law! The wicked, opportunist father-in-law, however, saw an opening to make a deft move. He would *'use'* his daughter's *in-love* experience as bait to secure David's death. He would name the dowry due to him from David as a hundred fore-skins of the Philistines. That way, the straddling young man would be entrapped. That was all the evil genius king's un-renewed mind had worked, *overdrive*, upon!

However, the Bible records that David *"behaved himself wisely in all his ways; and the LORD was with him."*[7] Saul had made a *huge* gaffe, again! Let all the hosts of hell scheme against a child of God; if God's abiding presence be with His child, hell should but fail! That reminder ought to make you shout and rejoice!

Instead of a hundred foreskins, David laid at the king's feet, double his asking price! *If you were Saul, tell, what gutted reaction would have greeted you at the sight of David's feat?*

I'd tell you of king Saul's reactions: *"And Saul saw and knew that the LORD was with David"*; and became yet *"more afraid of David; and Saul became David's enemy continually."*[8] Saul *saw* (conceived) and *knew* (perceived) of God's presence with David, yet he pursued him as drone, a target, to the detriment of his very own soul!

After a few years of her marriage to David, the son of Jesse; Michal, Saul's daughter began to throw tantrums in a blatant display of the *spirit of despise* against the anointed – much like her father, the king did. David demonstrated the "spirit of understanding." He tucked his hands into those very hands that govern the universe. He danced and rejoiced in the God of his salvation! Michal, however, became accursed – and died childless. She was the only known woman in the entire scriptures who had perished un-regenerative![9]

## Gaining Understanding in Inextricable Covenant Relationships

Let me offer you practical insight with which you will overcome the less-than-desirable situation you find yourself, particularly, if you are involved in an inextricable covenant relationship:

*First, being in a covenant relationship simply means you're bonded.* If in a marriage situation, we'd say you are "wedlock-ed." You are bound either by an oath, an agreement or a legal obligation from which you may *not* be expected to seek dissolution; take for instance, a marriage covenant.

*Second, you should not automatically jettison such a purulent covenant-relationship.* Doing so would *not* alleviate your plight. *Nabal-Abigail* covenant relationship types could only be terminated by God's miraculous intervention of *any* magnitude; the death of the errant party inclusively sealed as the last resort-option God could be *forced* to take.

Whichever way God chooses to settle the scroll, the righteous must keep their eyes upon the Lord!

*Third, seek intermediation and counsel.* Both parties ought to have a trained, trusted, marriage/relationship counselor or a pastor they both *must* mutually respect. You must make efforts to work at your relationship; the hurts, the disrespect and disagreements, not withstanding!

Listen, *there ain't no grass greener on the other side of the fence; if it looks greener, it would still require mowing!*

Book an appointment with your trusted professional christian counselor or pastor; you'd be wiser if you did! If you can't afford a *pro* – and the pastor has gone on holiday with his family, call one of the elders in the church. Or one of the elderly ladies in the church; you would be amazed the level of wisdom possessed by these godly, gentle ladies.

If you're un-churched, call for the trusted elderly man/woman who'd not mince words with you. Do *not* call someone who would want to only tell you what you would only want to hear!

Worthy of emphasis though, is the fact that when a party defaults in covenant matters, the defaulter automatically brings a reproach on the less guilty. But be comforted; I assuredly tell you, God shall surely bring the godly out of temptations and reserve the ungodly therein for punishment. 2 *Peter 2:9* confirms to us that:

> *"The Lord knoweth how to deliver the godly out of temptations and to reserve the unjust unto the day of judgment to be punished."*

*When would God's punishment of the unjust be due?*

The punishment of the unjust shall be due when God had fully exhausted all amicable ways to rescue the hitherto unconcerned, stiff-necked, damnable soul of the wicked:

> *"The Lord is not slack concerning his promise, as some men count slackness; but is longsuffering to us-ward, not willing that any should perish, but that all should come to repentance."*
>
> 2 Peter 3:9

## Demonstrating the "Spirit of Understanding" in Troubled Times

Let me show you from Abigail's life, practical demonstrations of this phenomenon called the "spirit of understanding."

I perfectly realize that we live in a fallen world – details of which are not hidden from God! Yet, with the exception of the biblical injunction mentioned by the Lord in *Matthew 13:9* – only upon the grounds of infidelity; that is, unfaithfulness/cheating on the part of one of the spouses – may the other instigate a divorce.

On the other hand, I am acutely aware that there are severe *red-route* lanes that would lead to the death of any marriage – but your duty it is to ensure that you do *not* trans-navigate those pernicious lanes. Such circumstances that will necessarily take you into the quicksands of marital death are inclusive of physical altercations, violations and aggravations; physical, mental, emotional and financial neglect and/or unreasonable behavior such as the denial of your spouse sexual intimacy (for a period of not lesser than six months); any abusive behavior, gambling, drunkenness, doping and drugging – and other conditions that may break, brutalize or lead to injury or threaten the life of a spouse shall be legally acceptable as legitimate grounds for the dissolution of an *irreparably* damaged marriage in today's divorce court of law.

Whatever reason(s) disagreeing couples have cited in divorce petitions, be aware of one resolute, unchanging truth that has been unequivocally stated by the Inventor of the marriage institution:

> *"For the LORD, the God of Israel saith that he hateth putting away: for one covereth violence with his garment, saith the LORD of hosts ..."*
>
> Malachi 2:16

If you do not believe that God *hates* divorce, fine; all you need do is ask someone who has been through one! (By the way, never believe a liar who tries to convince you saying of theirs: *"We had an amicable divorce."*) It was either *their* marriage was based on falsity and lies, or it was a union of convenience! There was no divorce that ever was amicable – particularly when children were involved!

Your spouse may be terminally ill! *Would you reckon it in your understanding, morally upright, to start seeing someone else behind their back, whilst you pay them lip-service?*

If you are still confused about what direction your change of heart should take on this issue, be human enough. Trade places with your spouse – albeit in your mind's eye! Be candid with your evaluation. Admit your conviction to your very self and God alone.

Abigail did not abscond from *her* matrimonial home. Neither did she abandon *her* marital obligations to Nabal; she knew there was - and is - a just and true Judge above, Who always vindicates. In the end, she was right!

The spirit of understanding demands that you:

*i.) Do not rush into marriage skipping the necessary period of courtship.* That is what the courtship period is meant for: discovery of your intended mate within appreciable and healthy boundaries. This period of discovery, I would recommend should not be lesser than six months – though an individual's willingness to "open-up" and avail themselves for discovery by another, varies from person to person.

*ii.) Do not get married without ensuring that both of you agree to a final authority guarding the code of acceptable behavior.* For the born again christian, their final authority lies in doing what they read in the Bible, God's holy Word! *(If your intending spouse isn't interested in reading to discover – and doing the Word of God with you in courtship, why on earth would they want to study and practice the Word with you when you are both married? Isn't that, actually, the first red-flag you should have noticed?)*

*iii.) Ensure you have trusted counselors, pastors and elders praying for you.* The Bible says: *"Where no counsel is, the people fall: but in the multitude of counsellors, there is safety."*[10]

*iv.) Ensure you do not resort to "silent treatment" i.e ignoring each other when you have an argument or disagreement in courtship/marriage.* Talk matters through – always eagerly attempting to sort things out between both of you, first. Schedule time to listen to each other – and hear each other well. Do not go to bed without settling *issues* of the day. Choose to forgive – and make allowances for the occurrence of errors. Do not tally your spouse's wrong-doings; you *ain't no copper*! (Even at that, cops sometimes do relent, in their powers to booking of an offence!)

*v.) Keep ALL third parties out of your disagreement matters.* "Third parties" have a way of magnifying issues, diversifying opinions, interests and attentions. "Third parties" are inclusive of your child(ren)/step-child(ren), blood relatives from both sides – and closest friends. Make your spouse your *best* friend and "first party", after God!

*vi.) Never threaten to leave your spouse; it demoralizes and genders unto distrust, anger, frustration and resentment of the 'abuser.'* Threatening separation from a spouse is a form of seeking power to control and manipulate the other, emotionally. It is a gross form of emotional abuse.

## A Case for Separation or Divorce

If you do not threaten, but must separate from them, spell out in no uncertain language the reason(s) for your decision. Express yourself in as easy-to-understand statement as: *"Jerry, I am leaving you because of your resolve not to undertake therapy to address your unreasonable behavior:* _____ *"* Name such irrational behavior they may be addicted to such as substance abuse, drinking, gambling away family's money, undue neglect, self-harm, violence and assault *etcetera*. You must remain firm, resolute and calm. Always have a second party with you for protection and need of witness, whilst you leave.

Now that they or you have left, you're now separated. Your separation at this time is still *not* a legal separation. You both will determine which direction to steer the marriage at this stage. A period of separation – whether legal or otherwise is an indication of the fact that your marriage is sick, and in a dire need of urgent attention and possibly, an *ICU* care.

Notice, even a legally separated spouse is still married! Hence, dating or *going out* with another person is ethically, morally, legally and spiritually wrong. It is called an affair!

*If you have attempted to reconcile your differences but the reconciliation attempts have proven abortive over time, keep praying and trusting God to touch and heal hearts, hurts and pains.* Then you shall remain married until there is a breakthrough – or a 'final fall apart.'

*If you get divorced, I would be sorry to learn of this unhealthy development.* But please never enter the rebound game; it's a sure way to bleed and lose again. And please, ensure that you do not become over-swallowed by guilt feelings. Seek the comfort and support of trusted friends and families.

Reflect on the pathways you have trod the entire time of your marriage. Divorce has never resulted from the sole actions of *a* spouse. Your reflective moments will bring conviction – and more, healing! Ensure you're nurtured back to health. Be healed spiritually, psychologically, financially and otherwise. Divorce does drain the *very* life of a person, regardless of how strong a personality they may be!

Purchase and read a copy of my book *"Before You Step into Someone Else's Shoes,"* published by PULSE Publishing House, U.K, 2010; ISBN 978-0-9567298-0-4, before you decide to make another crucial life decision.

## Wisdom in Other Troubled Times, Relationships and Mid –Life Crises

*i.) Do not disown your errant teenager child:*
Somehow we have found it easier to love an obedient child, haven't we? How do we handle a disobedient teen-aged child?

If you neglected, disowned or forsook your child when teenage hormones were raging, you would have caused them, almost, an irreparable emotional damage by the time their senses had returned to them, in latter years!

Parenting is a job signed for "until death." True parents do *not* stop caring for – and praying for that child, despite the heart-break he/she had caused.

Same goes for spiritual parents exercising authority over an errant son/daughter in the faith. Pray for them. Do *not* curse, though they deserved being accursed because of their unfaithful, dis-honoring conduct directed at you. No, wait for them patiently with the *agape* love of God; you will find them back at your doorstep after many days, months or even years! You *must* remain steadfast in love and forgiveness; this is what *true* parents practice!

*ii.) Do not evil entreat those who have maligned you:*
God brings people into our lives for a reason, for a season or for a lifetime. You must be spiritually aware for what reason God had brought *any* into your life.

Relationships go through many stages – including everything between hurts and offences, but also forgiveness and healings. If you have been abused, maligned or broken, intercede for those who have stolen or 'murdered' a part of you. David would not execute *'his master'*, king Saul, in revenge, even though the opportunity twice availed itself. [11] Instead, the anointed of God demonstrated his unshakeable innate understanding that God's long hands of vengeance will someday wrap itself in a tight grip round Saul's neck. He verbalized his convictions thus:

> *"David said furthermore, As the LORD liveth, the LORD shall smite him; or his day shall come to die; or he shall descend into battle and perish.*
>
> *The LORD forbid that I should stretch forth mine hand against the LORD's anointed ..."*
> 1 Samuel 26:10-11

*Isn't that what the Bible refers to as possessing "the spirit of understanding"?*

Like David, Abigail also possessed an understanding mind in that she would *not* sit back idly and watch evil befall Nabal – and the vast staffers that have made their enterprise grow so vast. That would have been a tragedy that wouldn't have begged for screaming headlines in Carmel town's leading tabloid newspapers and media! A possible headline would have read:

> **"Innocent Heads Rolled at Nabal Shearing & Dairy Farms alongside Wicked Boss', In an Onslaught by a Hungry General!"**

What a *savior* Abigail had been!

She had swiftly interceded and pleaded with wisdom before angry David to save the life of her husband Nabal –

*not* because Nabal loved her; but rather, because she possessed a perfect understanding of the terms of the marriage covenant.

*iii.) Know when to speak – and what to say:*
An astute woman filled with the *"spirit of understanding"*, Abigail had kept the details of her *"Rescue Mission"* a secret, away from Nabal's knowledge because she had a perfect control over the reins of her heart! She must have purposed and re-affirmed, time and again: *"I said, I will take heed to my ways, that I sin not with my tongue: I will keep my mouth with a bridle, while the wicked is before me."*[12]

By the spirit of understanding, Abigail knew that *any* who maligns, restrains or pursues with an intent to harm the anointed of the Lord, should have their souls slung out *"as out of the middle of a sling."*[13] (Sometimes, you reckon how folk could accurately foretell futuristic happenings; it is by the self-same *spirit of understanding!*) According to the *word of knowledge* spoken by Abigail, the "Righteous Judge" deemed fit that the *'angel of death'* should snuff life out of Nabal on, exactly, the tenth day of his cursing and railing on those ten fainting soldiers David had sent to him, to beseech his help![14]

*May such fate that had eventually befallen Haman, Herod Agrippa and Nabal become the lot of all the enemies of God's precious and anointed people now and forevermore. Amen.*

## Inextricable Relationship #2: Unhealthy Sibling Rivalry and Hatred – Joseph & His Ten Brothers

> *"But as for you, ye thought evil against me; but God meant it unto good, to bring to pass, as it is this day to save much people alive."*
>
> Genesis 50:20

Permit me to send a shudder through your being – and here is it: if you're a *gem*, you are featured on the devil's target-hit list!

The devil targets great potentials; his mindset is to have them sifted like the chaff of the wheat that they may *not* attain unto their destiny. But here's the *Goodnews*: if the devil failed to thwart Joseph's destiny, he will woefully fail on all his attempts to take you out, in the name of the Lord!

This sniper fella *really* did plot against Joseph's destiny in every way and at every turn. When Joseph turned a new bend, before he could gather momentum to pace the home stretch, the *giant of 'unfair victimization'* had hamstrung him at the Achilles'. This was the story of his foundational twenty-eight years, until *his day* arrived. *His day* ushered in God's blue-print design for *his* destiny. We shall later see the various victimizations Joseph endured. In the interim, however; let us understand what the name, *"Joseph"* meant.

## Digging Deeper

The name *"Joseph"* is a short prayer, meaning: *"Let Him Add."* A more accurate rendition of that name ought to be: *"Let God Add to Him."*

Now we understand that by Joseph's name and an earlier encounter with God, he had had an understanding that God would someday make him great as a deliverer – and a *savior*.

*Isn't that what prosperity really is: God's empowerment of one so as to empower and deliver another, or a people?*

Well, what information Joseph may *not* have been debriefed were the invariable great pains he would undergo to emerge as a preserver of men's lives. *Heaven will usually reveal a large expanse of vision, in parts; bit by bit, step by step, all the way!* Saul of Tarsus, converted, would be the only exception to this rule: he was foretold *"how great things he must suffer for my name's sake."*[15]

Joseph's rise to becoming the Prime Minister of Egypt was a successive story detailing fierce exposures to temptations of his will to succumb to lust for sexual gratification, power, selfishness and bitterness. The budding young man *had* to choose between the silkier alternatives of life and heading for God's excruciating character mould-blocks! Believe me, you and I are destined for the same route: God's mould-blocks await our arrival!

Not only would Joseph have to be sore tested, his destiny-track was to be spiritually engineered by variables completely outside his sphere of domain. He was always a victim until Providence *trumped* him victorious!

Let us consider some of the victimizations this untainted man of God endured.

## 11 Unfair Victimizations of Joseph

*1.) Joseph was a victim of his dad's favoritism and transferred love:*
Joseph was the eldest son of his father, Jacob's true love, Rachel, who hitherto was long barren. Jacob's other wives: Leah – whom he had been deceived to marry by his Uncle Laban – and Rachel's maids Bilhah and Zilpah had birthed him ten sons and a daughter before Joseph's arrival on the family scene.

Very soon afterwards, Rachel would die of child birth complications at her attempt delivering Benjamin, Joseph's only sibling!

Joseph, *"the son of Jacob's old age;"* who was at this time a half orphan, had had the love Jacob meant for Rachel, his mum, transferred onto him.[16] It was undeniably obvious: Papa had made *Joe*, a special *"coat of many colors."* When his half-brothers saw this, they hated *Joe* very passionately. *"They hated him, and could not speak peaceably unto him."*[17]

You have read it yourself; your preference of one child above the other(s) will pave the path for sibling rivalry and hatred.

*2.) Joseph was a victim, loving an unruly brotherhood:*
Joseph grew up in what we could call a mixed/blended family setting (in today's western context), and a fierce polygamous setting (in third world context). At any rate, his half-brothers were of a *wild caste* because the Bible attests in *Genesis 37:2* that they conducted their affairs with a spice of evil! The report Joseph had brought Dad was his capture of the images of their nefarious activities on the field!

*"… and Joseph brought unto his father their evil report."*

**3.) Joseph was a victim in reverse, of correctional mindedness:**
How often true it is that those whom we intend to correct and instruct in righteousness would soon begin to hate us. Joseph had the good of his brethren at the back of his mind when he brought a report to Dad! But he would become a victim in reverse!

**4.) Joseph was a victim of lack of psychological self restraint:**
Joseph's dominant character could best be described as *'sanguine'*; that is, *"a warm blooded, effervescent and bubbly, helpful, serviceable but chatter-box-like character."* Having many strong factors in their favor, one quickly traceable trait of weakness of people with dominant *sanguine* character is that they tend to *over-react emotionally* or *talk without restraints*, particularly when excited.

*Could it have been that Joseph's negative report to father Jacob of his siblings' activities was unwarranted?*

I personally submit that Joseph had over-encumbered his brethren with his words. And they *had* hated him!

He would however soon begin to learn to self-recreate, because there has never been *any* who achieved the pinnacle of the destiny God called had ear-marked for them, without bridling their tongue.

**5.) Joseph was a victim of spiritual gift exercise:**
Being endowed with extraordinary spiritual gifts is not enough. A visionary must exercise his gifts with utmost discerning. The people with whom to share, the time to share – and the environment to share the heavenly vision require a *release* in the spirit. You cannot possibly conquer this giant of victimization that so threatens your destiny, flagrantly flaunting my prescription.

Once flashed onto the screen of your mind, that vision must be kept within your decoder's monitoring device and code-locked until the safest opportunity to reveal it to the world arrives.

Saul, revealed as king through the mouth of Samuel would *not* in his sane mind divulge to his inquisitive Uncle the prophecy of his rulership of Israel.[18] If Saul's action here earned God's recommendation, it must be worthy of emulation!

Joseph had exercised his spiritual gifting in an immature way, and had paid dearly for this! He ended up being sold off by his audience:

> *"And they hated him yet the more for his dreams, and for his words."*
> Genesis 37:8

But while his brethren scoffed and breathed out cruelty, Father Jacob *"observed"* Joseph's prophecies.[19] Jacob's strict observance ought to be the reaction also, of godly parents who would not serve as objects of delay to their children's visions. Remember, Mary the mother of Jesus also had kept all of Jesus' *"sayings in her heart."*[20] Hence, it is part of godly parenting for parents/guardians to closely observe and monitor their children's *'sayings'*; until those *'sayings'* become actualized!

Now, if your child/ward has no *'sayings'*, you go ahead and verbalize some *'sayings'* over them!

6.) *Joseph was a victim of brethren's conflicting interest, evil plots, lies, malice and conspiracies:*

> *"And when they saw him afar off, even before he came near unto them, they conspired against him to slay him."*
> Genesis 37:18

Their long awaited day to *"mess with"* Joseph's destiny eventually arrived. Driven by rage, envy and age-long malice, they conspired to terminate his life. But God intervened, however, through the instrumentality of Reuben's counsel: he saved Joseph's life from their murderous plot.

We applaud Ruben. Most of us thought his motives for performing this heroic salvation act were *very* laudable. Ah, not quite! Come with me.

Scripture declares in *Genesis 35:22* that Reuben had an incestuous relationship with Bilhah, the youngest of Jacob's wives! This wicked deed automatically waived away from him, the rights of the first born son – which entitled every first born male in the Jewish culture of that time, to a double portion of his father's inheritance. But Ruben had sinned against his own soul; his rightful double apportionment, his step-mother, Bilhah – and against his father, Jacob.

But wait; there was still one more person whose forgiveness he deeply craved.

As this incestuous incontinence was committed after the death of Rachel, it wouldn't be just a crime committed against Jacob and Bilhah alone; it could be rightly regarded as an affront well directed against Joseph too, since Bilhah was logically, Joseph's step-mother. Hence, Bible scholars are not unmindful that Reuben's act of saving Joseph from death was an attempted showy piece of evidence of his external penitence for his earlier affront and vicious attack.

A very shrewd *act*, Ruben:

- inwardly coveted to have restored unto himself the first born rights and privileges. (Those rights and privileges, however, wouldn't ever be his nor Judah's – but the righteous man sold as a slave to the Midianites!);

- contrived, inwardly, to attempt to convince father Jacob with his supposed, re-gained sense of responsibility, through his magnanimity towards Joseph: the evident proof of this would be the pit slime that had smeared his garments; and finally, Ruben;

- intended to have convinced Joseph of his support and love for him (which he genuinely did *not* possess), in order to have earned his forgiveness for violating his step-mom.

7.) *Joseph was a victim of brethren's cold rejection:*
The fear of rejection or neglect – particularly by loved ones and blood relations could spark the on-start of mental agony and torture, depression, love-sickness, psychological traumas and various other dysfunctions – not forgetting to mention, possibly, insanity in *any* so rejected.

*Are you undergoing rejection at the moment?*

If so, receive the comforting, re-assuring, healing love of God that *you are loved and highly valued* by Him, right now in Jesus' wonderful name.

Joseph's brethren's act of rejection was a clue of their cruel and murderous intents! Once they had thrown him into the pit, they had the peace in their mischievous little hearts to nurse their fleshly desires. The Bible categorically states that *"they sat down to eat bread."*[21]

God's word teaches that there is an inherent curse reserved for those who can ill-afford to dwell at ease in Zion. This interprets, God frowns at folk who are so apathetically indifferent to others' plights, having *"not grieved for the affliction of Joseph."*[22]

**8.) Joseph was a victim of a "sell off":**
Before Reuben's return to the company later in the day, Joseph had been sold as a slave to the Ishmeelites. Take this: whenever anyone had initiated an action on behalf of a group – having *not* received authority to act from the spiritual, moral or physical leader, and having *not* been delegated with such powers to act; such action *should* never be bleached of error. Such a person, too, would be held in the *very* wrong!

A couple of instances in the Word of God bear witness to this truth. First, king Saul had been judged to be in the wrong – and had lost his rulership the moment he had gored into the *priestly office* and offered a sacrifice unto the Lord on behalf of Prophet Samuel.[23] Second, Nadab and Abihu had been stricken dead at the altar embers of which they had stoked when they had offered a *"strange fire before the LORD."* Nobody had even mourned their demise![24]

Now, the proceeds of any *'sell-off'* are the price of blood!

Such proceeds cannot and must *not* be deemed as acceptable offerings before the altar of the living God! For instance, the wages of *"body sale"*, the Bible refers to as *"the hire of a whore"* or *"the price of a dog"* in *Deuteronomy 23:18*.

These days, some self-professed pastors accept offerings from whatever quarters and means to further the work of *their* ministry. Rightly said, these are not God's ministries

– they are men's. Consequently, such men's works shall undoubtedly suffer the libation fire of He Who calls Himself: *"the Consuming fire."*[25]

*'Sell–off'* history is quite traceable in biblical history. In Prophet Joel's days, parents with a numb conscience had *'sold'* a daughter for a bottle of wine and pimped a son – if he was fortunate enough to have escaped being offered in a practical burnt offering to the monstrous horse-man god, Molech.[26] Esau, Joseph's uncle had *'sold'* his birthright to the better than he for a plate of meal.[27] Judas, the betrayer, had *'sold'* Jesus Christ the Righteous One, for mere thirty pieces of silver![28]

*Are you currently involved in a 'deal', or a 'sell-off' of a close friend or family member?*

'Sell-off' does *not* always involve trading in money proceeds: whenever you have intentionally, wickedly ignored, neglected, and deliberately "hands-off" the vulnerable as to open the door for evil to befall them, you are guilty of not discharging your duty to protect and preserve the less able.

But Joseph had been *'sold'* into slavery for twenty of pieces silver. This was the *basest* negotiable price he could fetch at the moment. He would further fetch the Ishmeelite merchants, a greater gain in another *'sell-off'* to Portiphar, in a few years' time.

*And what do you opine Joseph's brothers had done with the proceeds of his sale?*

Because they were ruled by their *flesh*, they possibly had eaten and gotten drunk – and probably had had a fight sharing the rest of the money. This was *why* later in life, they had inevitably been ravished by famine! Revisit with me Prophet Jeremiah's words of the consequence to anyone who dealt harshly with, tormented or shed the blood of an anointed, innocent person:

> *"But know ye for certain, that if ye put me to death, ye shall surely bring innocent blood upon yourselves, and upon this city, and upon the inhabitants thereof ..."*
> Jeremiah 26:15

Jesus' blood unjustly shed consigned the nation of Israel – up until this day – onto the dark period of severance from a deeper understanding of God. This was that which Prophet Jeremiah had spoken of as the time of *"Jacob's trouble"* – though, ironically; this period works the procurement of the Gentiles' peace![29]

**9.) Joseph was a victim of parental old age loneliness-onslaught:** Care-giving is a major *real* issue we should be more than ready to grapple with. We live in a system that is finding it increasingly tougher to cater for our elderly citizens!

*So who should care for the elderly?*

The older citizenry certainly do *not* want to be a burden of any sort to the younger! But just as the thinning of the crown or temple hair-lines in men in their middle-aged years or the menopause and its flushes in women in latter years; growing old must be embraced and accepted as another graceful, natural stage in the cycle we call *"life."*

I know some people, my age, who dread getting old; but I cannot wait to receive this blessing of the Lord upon myself – and my loved ones, including you! And before my pen diverts, the question remains:

*"Who should care for the elderly?"*

I believe the answer to this question lies with the elderly-to-be, first and foremost! The virile, active, aged *18-65 workforce group* can best begin to re-orientate their thought patterns of youthful years evidenced by their lifestyles, to reflect the kind of care *they* would love to receive when they become old. The way we pattern and invest our youth, inevitably, *should* be our expectation of returns on how we would spend our aged years.

*Would you love to learn of my advice on the question of care for the elderly?*

The answer is in one summative word: I-N-V-E-S-T!

Invest and plan for old age *now*, while you are young and able! Make strong efforts to invest where it matters. Invest in God and in the things of God. Invest in the people God has placed in your life: *your* spouse and child(ren) – if you have them! Friends and families - nuclear and extended! As has been well summarized by Maya Angelou:

> *"Each child belongs to all of us and they will bring us a tomorrow in direct relation to the responsibility we have shown them."*

The people in our lives are the first basic, rightful investments we all must endeavor to put strong efforts into. These are the kinds of investments that most matter. Refuse to let any disagreement wedge a wall of divide between you and your loved ones: parents, children, siblings, friends, workmates *etcetera* – ir-respective of that level of discord. Always find a way to mend the bridges. Forgive, restore – and forgive again!

Aged people *may* become prone to loneliness. In the first chapter, I identified the loneliness that people suffer in old age: a kind of an expectation of another life, much fuller than that they currently live! This loneliness cannot be cured with money, riches, lands or fame.

Jacob in old age was *not* poor. But somehow, he only recently realized the truth about the loneliness of the aged. He allowed his emotions to get wrapped up with his old, treacherous scheming ways of youth. A few tragedies helped accentuate this imbalance in his feelings: his most beloved wife, Rachel had died in her prime; his first son Ruben had uncovered his skirt, his first daughter Dinah had been uncouthly – and had ended up being defiled by Prince Shechem the Hivite, a heathen![30] All of Jacob's other sons had been most unruly – except *same* Joseph and his younger brother, Benjamin! Joseph therefore was the only trustworthy one in whom Jacob had relished – and upon whom his soul and sole-companionship depended.

In developing countries where there are not in place governmental care facility programs, adequate forecast and preparations ought to be made for the care and companionship of aged parents by ALL the children. This responsibility should not be abandoned to the one caring child available, who surely would become so burdened and encumbered with such enormous responsibilities that are meant to be shared by the whole family.

Thank God for the young carers here in the United Kingdom; I salute the huge sacrifices you have made towards the well-being of your parents, siblings – and loved ones. But again, I suggest that highlights of carers' plights and remunerations should be given more prominence in the national planning and budgets than currently are.

Advanced parents must *not* present proneness to loneliness as a tool of manipulation on *any* child; naturally, God designed it that children owe it a sense of duty and responsibility to their parents to cater for them not just in old age but at all times. So as a child, stop incurring upon your head, unspoken parental curses due to your neglect of the father and mother who gave you life. Take good care of your parents – whether young, middle-aged, ageing or aged.

Understandably, Jacob had exploited the youthfulness, willingness and singleness of *the* responsible, kind-hearted Joseph to comply with his lack of appropriate companionship. Joseph had been victimized – even by the *very* father who very much loved him.

10.) *Joseph was a victim of a 'sexed-up' sexual allegation:*
If you were Joseph, wouldn't you have thought that there was a curse on your life – particularly whenever you were just about to settle down to what you were good at; something pretty horrible suddenly unsettles you. "Am I not battling with a curse?"; this seems the normal thought line you would have towed! There in Egypt, in his master's house, dedicatedly going about his assigned duties as a *'sold'* slave, Joseph would again become a victim of his boss' wife's intense sexual advances and threats!

What mind could have conceived of such dastardly act from Mrs. Portiphar? Not Joseph's, in the very least! So righteous Joseph turned down the over-sexed giant's requests to come and be defiled! *He continued his daily routine with opened eyes!* Day after day still, her offers came, unstopped. God was looking. Angels were watching. The man of God was being passed through God's furnace without which he couldn't have been rightly moulded for the governance of Egypt!

After Joseph had persistently refused her suggestive advances, Mrs. Portiphar could no longer contain both the urge and the insults brought about by Joseph's continued resistance. She *had* to make a move:

> "And it came to pass about this time, that Joseph went into the house to do his business; and there was none of the men of the house there within.
>
> And she caught him by his garment, saying, Lie with me: and he left his garment in her hand, and fled, and got him out ..."
> Genesis 39:11-12

In today's world, for *sexting*, sexual harassment, pestering, molesting – and an eventual assault on a *'bond worker'*, Joseph would be rightly counseled to sue Mrs. Portiphar. There would surely have been some *CCTV* footages to corroborate the truth – followed by a heavy compensation or injury payout award against the aggressor, Mrs. Portiphar.

Instead, the impudent-faced Mrs. Portiphar turned the tide against Joseph and got him *'framed'*. Joseph, once again became a victim of the crime of an evil conscience. Joseph's alleged crime carried the heftiest penalty, the death sentence, in the Egypt of that day.

If you were Joseph, what would have been going through your mind? Wouldn't you have queried: *'God, is this how You reward a faithful saint's perseverance to live holy?'*

Having listened to the rants of his wife, Captain Portiphar detained Joseph in jail until his execution papers would be filed and served. But he will sleep over the matter: the ultimate decision to snuff Joseph's life, entirely at the disposal of the troubled husband! He downed a glass of wine – and then proceeded to bed.

Then God intervened; yet again! Portiphar could *not* sleep.

The Joseph Portiphar knew had been faithful, God had been with him; practically everything had flourished under him.[31]

*There seems to be a mistake, somewhere,* he reasoned.

Still dazed, the Captain called the *Home Office* and asked that Joseph Jacob's *Residence of Abode Letter* be rescinded. He would serve time – and after this, be deported to Edom!

Joseph had escaped the executor's blade. Somehow, by the Hands that guide providence, he had also escaped been sent to Egypt's Maximum Security Prison, Cairo. Instead, he would serve time with Pharaoh's top political detainees:

> *"And Joseph's master took him, and put him into the prison, a place where the king's prisoners were bound: and he was there in the prison."*
> Genesis 39:20

Once behind close doors, methinks Satan thought it all finished; thus went on a holiday on Joseph's case. That has always been his thought pattern![32] But such crucial times are the times God reaches for His *'super charged turbo'* buttons: the invisible hands of the Creator of men's destinies were busy carving out a niche for His most celebrated prisoner of all times.

Portiphar life-jailed Joseph and thought it for a punitive demotion to the slave; God planned His servant's jail-experience for a promotion. Portiphar thought Joseph would become a *statistic*; God meant Joseph to become a global *fact* to be reckoned with in the world of his days. Joseph had become a *political prisoner*, closest to his breakthrough – closest to the crest of Egypt's political seat of power.

Yet God would not spare his gem the tiniest spot; He would still apply the refiner's fire! Joseph would still fall, yet another victim!

*11.) Joseph was a victim of broken trust by a potential helper:* One phrase you would find recurring all through the story of Joseph is: *"But the LORD was with Joseph ..."* (Genesis 39:21). Whenever I have read the story of Joseph, and have come across that phrase, I have always loved to render it in two parts, thus: *"But the Lord", "... with Joseph!"*

The secret of Joseph's deliverance was that the Lord always showed up when all hopes had been but lost: Joseph had learned to always secure the presence of the LORD! God's steadfast faithfulness would yet open another door unto Joseph, if he would engage his innate gifting.

These past eleven years, Joseph's spiritual gift of interpreting of dreams had been very dormant since the urgency at hand required the use of his physical strengths. *Hence, when physical strength must be engaged, divine strength must be disengaged. And vise versa!*

Yet in prison – and because he was an inquisitive man of compassion, Joseph's gift would again be in demand. He so genuinely much cared for the well being of his other inmates to the extent that they would confide in him. He would be requested to interpret the dreams of the offending chief Butler and Baker to Pharaoh!

According to Joseph's interpretation, the butler had been restored, and the baker, executed.

It should be a counselor's delight to receive counselees voluntarily returning to share with them, the testimonies of breakthroughs – and possibly, with a thanksgiving or appreciation *seed*; appreciating God's grace upon them! *'Counselees'* may also of their very accord render acts of benevolence to the Servant of God. This is Heaven's acceptable order. The counselor ought *not* present to counselees, *any* help requests, whatsoever! Neither should they make testifiers feel indebted to their recourse on the anointing.

But under the heat of the Refiner's fire, our dear brother Joseph almost at a breaking point, he'd actually kissed God's protocol: *b – y – e!* He had pleaded with the chief Butler:

> "But think on me when it shall be well with thee, and shew kindness, I pray thee, unto me, and make mention of me unto Pharaoh, and bring me out of this house;
>
> For indeed I was stolen away out of the land of the Hebrews: and here also have I done nothing that they should put me into the dungeon."
>
> Genesis 40:14-15

## *Victim Becomes Victor: Joseph Achieves his Destiny*

God would not share his glory with anyone! You would be heart broken *if* you serve God and flesh, at the same time.

A further two-year delay stint was slammed upon Joseph while Heaven's erasers promptly wiped clean the Chief Butler's remembrance and offer of help unto him:

*"Yet did not the chief butler remember Joseph, but forgat him."*
Genesis 40:23

God himself would bring Joseph out of prison into the palace – and *not* another!

As I approach the end of Joseph's story, I see a man of God without blemish, sent ahead – and pleased of the Lord to be bruised with afflictions in order to have God's people preserved.

*What length, width or height would you reckon God would be unwilling to go in order to have you prepared for your divine assignment?*

*"He sent a man before them, even Joseph, who was sold for a servant:*

*Whose feet they hurt with fetters: he was laid in iron:*

*Until the time that his word came: the word of the Lord tried him."*
Psalms 105:17-19

Man could have wronged Joseph. Circumstances could have blown him an ill wind; but in all of these, Joseph saw God alone initiating His divine counsel.

In the fullness of time, he was re-united with his Father and his kid brother, Benjamin. He bore the burdens of his half brothers and their families in his heart. He *chose* to forgive all those who offended him. He calmed his brothers' agitated minds. He had preserved a whole race. He had fulfilled his destiny. Joseph had only acted *his* apportioned part in birthing the destiny of the nation of Israel, the Messiah, and even *you!*

Making impact in your generation – and future generations by conscious decisions and choices is what living a meaningful life is about.

*Chapter 6*

# The Four Clans of Giants *en route* Canaan

*"If you want a place in the sun, you've got to put up with a few blisters."*
— Abigail Van Buren

Giants are synonymous with the hurdles and often harsh, unexpected challenging realities that suddenly confront us in life! They come in different sizes and shapes. Now, if you haven't faced any challenges yet, something must be drastically lacking in your destiny's fulfillment! I assuredly say this because encountering – and conquering giants is *the* surest way you would be re-assured that you are on the right pathway to Canaan. Encountering giants re-affirms which kingdom you belong to – and enforces the fact that you are a potential threat to the evil, retrogressive kingdom of Satan and his hell.

Giants ultimately stand between us and God's beautiful promises unto us. Their intent: to conquer us. Our intent, to defeat them! If you fail to overpower your giants, it is not attributable to any other reason but the littleness of your strength!¹ However, victorious conquerors receive extra spiritual nourishment from slaying *their* giants.²

We already noted four giants in the lives of the most pronounced delay sufferers in biblical times. How the patriarchs fought and overcame their challenges should become a worthy concern for *any* who would inherit *their* Canaan.

## *Origin and Clans of Giants*

Read carefully our study text in *Numbers Chapter Thirteen*, you will recognize the *origin* of the giants. Let us read in particular, *verses twenty-one and twenty-two:*

> *"So they went up, and searched the land ...*
>
> *And they ascended by the south, and came unto Hebron; where Ahiman, Sheshai, and Talmai, the children of Anak, were ..."*

From the scriptural verses above, therefore, we notice that the giants *en route* Canaan were descendants of Anak! *Numbers 13:33* refers to them as "the sons of Anak":

> *"And there we saw the giants, the sons of Anak, which come of the giants ..."*

However, the earliest reference of the origin of giants is found in *Genesis Chapter Six*. Here, fallen angels took upon themselves human semblance and intermarried with the unwary females. The product was humans with indomitable strength, in-exterminable fierceness and strangeness! These *new species* of humankind were so fierce and dominant, that they became *"mighty men which were of old, men of renown."*³

The whole of God's creature became polluted. This great wickedness angered God – *"and the Lord regretted that He had made man on the earth, and he was grieved at heart."*[4]

God was grieved because mankind, His prime creature now had acquired an additional genetic coding: new genes, demonically-modified by the diabolic machinery of hell. Henceforth, mankind would be perennially troubled by a strangeness from hell that would almost be hard to exterminate. Strange happenings: untraceable illnesses, inexplicable misfortunes, acute barrenness, afflictions and excruciating poverty to mention just a few, *would* plague mankind. Man would become fruitless, empty and wasted. Earth would become intolerable for its inhabitants. That was the sole aim of Satan – and his fallen angels who were expelled from Heaven.

Barrenness of all sorts was introduced into the womb of the earth through the giants' sexual defilement of our earlier mothers. It was the defiling semen of the hated species.

But the Redeemer God also had a redemptive plan for His seduced but much loved ace creature – mankind! He would introduce His *Seed*, into the womb of the Virgin Mary – in the fullness of times – to re-create a stronger, overcomer-strain that nothing in Heaven or on Earth, or in the water-world would be able to resist. Anyone who dares take upon him/herself the genetic codes of God's *Seed* would become invincible over the giants' plague – barrenness and all of the devil's atrocities!

The giants in the bible had their other tribes in *Ahiman, Sheshai* and *Talmai*. In latter years, David would engage and defeat Goliath of *Gath*.

In a similar token, today's giants you confront have their clans traceable to four major sources vis-à-vis:

- *spiritual numbness, strange incurable illnesses that defy medical know-how;*

- *protracted financial delays, closed door-encounters, unfavorable dispositions;*

- *unfulfilling relationships and the irrevocable consequences such relationships bring; and finally,*

- *excruciating physical barrenness, and ministerial/vocational delays and/or diversions!*

## God's Redemptive Purpose

> *"Thou shalt be blessed above all people: there shall not be male or female barren among you, or among your cattle.*
>
> *And the LORD will take away from thee all sicknesses, and will put none of the evil diseases of Egypt, which thou knowest, upon thee; but will lay them upon all them that hate thee.*
>
> *And thou shalt consume all the people which the LORD thy God shall deliver thee; and thine eye shall have no pity upon them ... "*
>
> Deuteronomy 7:14-16

God's redemptive purpose was to bring the Israelites to enter into and *possess* Canaan. Canaan symbolizes a fulfilled destiny.

When God swore to Israel: *"Thou shalt be blessed above all people: there shall not be male or female barren among you, or among your cattle"*, He had in mind an encompassing, total liberation of His beloved people. Not only would their spiritual and economic well being be His priority, their physical and relational domination would be guaranteed. That word *"blessed"* means to be *"supernaturally empowered to be productive, prosper, enlarge, become rich and dwell in health."*

## Understanding Barrenness

To further understand the *modus operandi* of the giants, we need to lay hold upon the original root word from which bareness sprouted. This word in the original tongue is called *aqar*.

*'Aqar'* has several derivates! It could mean:

- *to uproot by the roots, so that death follows. Literally this covers all cases of abortion, but could also be extended to cover the abortion of a dream, vision or purpose of a thing;*

- *to hamstring; for example, a horse so as to paralyze or inhibit movement;*

- *to cause to be sterile, the generative organs, and;*

- *to hold back, dam up or store away as to cause a delay.*

Now by the word of the Lord this day, I prophesy unto you that the end result of that strong giant's restraining influence you have experienced over the years would translate into a mighty release of bundles of blessings and joy in Jesus' mighty name! You get ready: *your* dam is about to burst its banks, momentously! I decree this season, your season of fruitfulness in Jesus mighty name! That delay – the court case, the immigration proceedings, the protracted illness, the siege on your finances and growth, your waiting period for *the* right spouse; all of *these things* will work for your ultimate good in the name of the Lord!

> *"And we know that all things work together for good to them that love God, to them who are the called according to his purpose."*
> Romans 8:28

Now, if we be *"the called"* according to God's purpose, it is mandatory, our lives must be conducted in the strictest adherence to His perfect will irrespective of the giant or the clan of the giant we engage in battle.

Thus, barrenness types could be portrayed via these four personalities:

*i.)* Joseph – personalized in protracted financial delays, numerous denials, threats of overthrowing a destiny;

*ii.)* Nabal & Abigail – personalized in irrevocable unfulfilling relationships;

*iii.)* Hannah – personalized in excruciating physical barrenness, and;

*iv.)* Apostle Paul and the Macedonian Call – personalized in ministerial or vocational delay and/or diversions!

Continuing from the preceding chapter, I have considered in much detail, teachings surrounding the lives of Mr. & Mrs. Nabal and Joseph!

Shall I then begin herewith, the process of understudying the other two personalized giants in the lives of Hannah and Apostle Paul?

## Hannah's Overcoming Physical Barrenness

*"And her adversary also provoked her sore, for to make her fret, because the LORD had shut up her womb."*

1 Samuel 1:6

Hannah's name translates *"favor"* or *"grace."* She was a perfect symbolic expression of grace in the midst of thorns – especially in the *ugly* face of sore provocation! Hannah's triumphant story over the demoralizing effects of physical barrenness and her testimonial song jubilating divine intervention are set out in *1 Samuel 1:1 - 2:10*

Now, Hannah was married to a man who deeply loved her despite the fact that she was unable to bear him a child. And this condition alone, by the culture of that time, left much to be desired of their marriage. Childlessness was a stain. In that culture, children were the proof; the basis and the legitimacy of *any* marriage.

It is so unfortunate however, that there are still cultures that hold the same view of the ancient Jews up until this day. In some parts of Africa, South East Asia, and Latin America, the husband's family may make life unbearable for the childless wife. Some marriages have been ruined because of the lack of *proof* of a child. Let me suggest these comforting words to you who have found yourself in a childless-couple setting:

• One, know that the inability to conceive at a period in time does *not* necessarily equal barrenness. With this medical fact in place;

- Second, recognize it is your rightful duty as the husband, to shield your wife – and *not* expose her to such ridicules, verbal and emotional attacks from *"concerned"* family members and friends who may appear so erstwhile concerned.

- Third, men whose wives have not been able to conceive and bear children must make additional adjustments to cater for their wives' emotional stability and well being through much love and re-assurances. Re-assure *your* wife repeatedly that all is well – *and mean it!* Stay faithful to watch over *your* home – and the well-being of *your* wife. Stay faithful and committed to *your* vows!

The source of Hannah's torment however, was *not* from her husband nor her husband's families, but the other woman in her man's life:

> "... *and Peninnah had children, but Hannah had no children.*"
> Verse 2

The rivalry was *very* rife. Peninnah taunted Hannah until her nerves jagged! Scripture captured this fact:

> "*And her adversary also provoked her sore, for to make her fret ...*"
> Verse 6

## *How Hannah Overcame Her Delay Being Fruitful*

A reaction is the body's management-response to pain or pleasure. Let me shed some light on helpful insights into how Hannah's reactions to her unfruitfulness made her triumphant:

**1.) Hannah recognized the source of the unfruitfulness:**
The Scripture says of Hannah in *1 Samuel 1:6* that: *"... the LORD had shut up her womb."* To enable you wage the rightful spiritual warfare, *you* must come to grips with the truthfulness of the source of *your* delay – and acknowledge it wholeheartedly unto the Lord without shame, regret or fear of reprisal.

Acknowledging the source of your challenge is a strong index of your stepping out from behind stagnation onto the super-highway of fruitfulness.

**2.) Hannah looked up unto the hills for help:**

*Where do you look unto in the heat of battle?*

Hannah did *not* run from pillar to post. We never heard that she did consult mediums! She did not even answer back her tormentor's hues and jeers. Neither did we see her transfer the irritable reaction of her possible frustration onto the children of her tormentor. She was never recorded as having been unreasonable or touchy! Her husband, Elkanah, intimated us of her disposition:

> *"Then said Elkanah her husband to her, Hannah, why weepest thou? and why eatest thou not? and why is thy heart grieved?"*
>
> 1 Samuel 1:8

If in a day of distress you attend to *life* with the disposition of a laughing gas; *"eating, drinking and merry-making"* like the Epicureans, you should not expect to receive Hannah's type of breakthrough!

Learn from Hannah: days of distress command some measure of sobriety.

3.) *Hannah was insatiable with Elkanah's gift of "a worthy portion," neither his offering of assurance of love that was "better than ten sons"'*:
Nothing on earth would replace Hannah's strong desire for *"a man child"*: this was the thirst and hunger of her soul! Treats, holidays and gift exchanges between a couple are great, but nothing should becloud the vision you have received of the Lord of conceiving *your child* of promise. (And when I say *"child of promise,"* I am *not* limiting that phrase to physical children alone; your *visions, dreams* and *aspirations* would also be regarded as *"children of promise"*).

Do not let good times drown your thirst for your *"child of promise."*

4.) *Hannah moved closer to God and attended worship services more regularly despite her 'barrenness'*:
Moving closer to God – and worshipping Him in a fruitless state of being may be tough; but that's exactly how *your Samuel* – *"child of promise"* – will be born! Drawing closer to God in times of affliction is a sign of strength, and not weakness. Wasn't this Prophet Habakkuk's reaction when the fig tree refused to blossom and there were no fruits on the vine – and the flock in the stall were cut off?[5]

Quality joy that rejoices the heart cannot be discovered through any other substituted means other than that which only is found available in the presence of God. *"Thou wilt show me the path of life: in thy presence is fullness of joy; at thy right hand there are pleasures forevermore."*[6]

5.) *Hannah would often tarry back at Shiloh to have some time of personal communion with God – when others have departed for their homes*:

Hannah had reached a place of alone with God without which no man achieves the inner strength that propels him unto greatness.

> *"So Hannah rose up after they had eaten in Shiloh, and after they had drunk. Now Eli the priest sat upon a seat by a post of the temple of the LORD.*
>
> *And she was in bitterness of soul, and prayed unto the LORD, and wept sore."*
>
> 1 Samuel 1:9-10

*6.) Hannah prayed purposefully:*

Be specific when you pray; pray according to the scriptures.

> *"And she ... said, O LORD of hosts ... look on the affliction of thine handmaid, and remember me, and not forget thine handmaid, but give unto thine handmaid a man child ..."*
>
> 1 Samuel 1:11

*7.) Hannah cut a covenant with the Lord of Hosts:*

> *"And she vowed a vow, and said O LORD of hosts, if thou wilt indeed look on the affliction of thine handmaid, and remember me, and not forget ... but wilt give unto thine handmaid a man child, then I will give him unto the LORD all the days of his life, and there shall no razor come upon his head."*
>
> Verse 11

Would you please notice two important lessons here?

First, a vow is a covenant, and;

Second, this afflicted woman shifted the battle gear from praying unto *EL-SHADDAI*, to praying unto *JEHOVAH SABOATH!*

Her deliberate, action-packed prayer is punctuated with sharp emphasis to a keen mind. Do not under-rate Hannah's superb intention here! She had appealed her case from a civilian point of view to the militaristic Commander-in-Chief of the Heavenly Hosts, the all time War General Who had never lost a battle – and would never lose one!

*'El-Shaddai' means the All-Sufficient God; the God who alone has all sufficiency! 'Jehovah Sabaoth' on the other hand means The LORD of HOSTS.*

*What service did she expect 'Jehovah Sabaoth' to render her?*

She expected the Commander of the Heavenly hosts to avenge her of her tormentor's boos and jeers – and *not forget* to open her womb to be able to conceive a *choice* male child!

*Dare you pray like Hannah, too?*

I do know that God never releases the *'Samuel's'* without first receiving the cries of the *'Hannah's.'* You too can cut a covenant with the Lord of Hosts, tied around your specific soul request.

8.) *Hannah continued steadfast in prayer:*
Do not relent. Even if the answer tarries, continue to pray! It surely shall soon *"come to pass."*

> *"And it came to pass, as she continued praying before the LORD, that Eli marked her mouth ...*
>
> *Then Eli answered and said, Go in peace: and the God of Israel grant thee thy petition that thou hast asked of him."*
>
> 1 Samuel 1:12, 17

You already know the rendition of the *Amplified Version* of the Holy Bible of *Matthew 7:7-8*; it places the key verbs in the present continuous: *"Ask and keep on asking ..."* it says. You also should never be wary of continually petitioning the Father, until your joy is full!

9.) *Believe the pronouncements the prophet of God presiding over you has proffered upon you and brighten your countenance accordingly:*

> *"Then Eli answered and said, Go in peace: and the God of Israel grant thee thy petition that thou hast asked of him.*
>
> *"So the woman went her way, and did eat, and her countenance was no more sad."*
>
> 1 Samuel 17-18

10.) *Do not abate praise despite answered prayers:*

> *"And they rose up in the morning early, and worshipped before the LORD ..."*
>
> 1 Samuel 1:19

11.) *Perform the actual fulfillment of your vow to God:*

> *"And they slew a bullock, and brought the child to Eli."*
>
> 1 Samuel 1:25

*12.) Share your testimony publicly:*
Your testimony shared publicly gives strength to the faith of other believers. Given, some will be jealous and angry; yet Heaven encourages you to strengthen other brethren once you have been strengthened.

Elkanah and Hannah stood before Eli and the whole congregation of Israel in Shiloh with the little baby Samuel in Hannah's arms. Peninnah, the tormentor and aggressor was conspicuously out of sight; nobody could care more about her whereabouts. She had faded into obscurity.

Pain gave way to joy as Hannah disclosed to the Prophet:

> *"Oh my lord, as thy soul liveth, my lord, I am the woman that stood by thee here, praying unto the LORD.*
>
> *For this child I prayed; and the LORD hath given me my petition which I asked of Him.*
>
> *Therefore also I have lent him to the LORD; as long as he liveth he shall be lent unto the LORD."*
> 1 Samuel 1:26-28

*13.) Burst forth singing; sing to the Lord of Hosts:*
Hannah sang thus singing and rejoicing before the LORD of Hosts:

> *"My heart rejoiceth in the LORD, mine horn is exalted in the LORD: my mouth is enlarged over mine enemies; because I rejoice in thy salvation."*
>
> *"There is none holy as the LORD: for there is none beside thee: neither is there any rock like our God."*
> 1 Samuel 2:1-2

*14.) Be unshakable in faith that you will again conceive other children:*

> *"And the LORD visited Hannah, so that she conceived, and bare three sons and two daughters. And the child Samuel grew before the LORD."*
>
> 1 Samuel 2:21

As I draw the curtains on Hannah's reverberating triumphant story over her childlessness, I want you to bear in mind, one crucial truth. That truth is that her crucial conception delay was engineered by the hands of the *very* God in Whose hands alone lie the times and seasons of the sons and daughters of men![7]

*If God cannot do evil, why then would He shut Hannah's womb?*

This question is one to which no theologian may be able to proffer an easy answer!

While God cannot do evil, we have found throughout scriptures that anyone who has avowed to follow Him *may* be subject to the most harrowing tests and tribulations. But these tribulations and afflictions will in the end, eventually lead to promotion. In Hannah's case, her *seed*; the fruit of her womb would become *the* child unto whom generations yet unborn would make a point of reference. Samuel would be the bridge between the old and the new orders of prophets and priests forevermore! That lone reason for Hannah's delay in fruitfulness is, in hindsight, a very worthy cause!

## *Overcoming Ministerial Confusion, Delay or Diversion: Paul's Call to Macedonia*

Apostle Paul's ministry to the Gentile world would *not* have materialized had the Macedonian vision *not* been relayed by Heaven. This story is told in *Acts 16*.

Heading towards Macedonia was a major diversion away from the well-charted second missionary journey of Paul and his team; but even, this launch-pad into their ministerial fulfillment was birthed in a serious crisis. Godly success in ministry has always been preceded by excellent crises management and curtailment skills. These skills are imparted by the Holy Spirit – much like a software is downloaded unto a computerized appliance. The Chinese probably understands better the word *"crisis"*, than anyone else upon the face of the earth. *"Crisis"*, to him, translates: *"opportunity in the midst of dangers."*

Ancient Antioch in Syria was Paul's launch-pad. *Acts 15* was the crisis point of his evangelistic ministry. *Acts 16* was the turning point. Whatever actions were recorded between those two chapters are what I would refer to as the *'crises management/curtailment skills'* that would prove eventful; if thoroughly deployed.

Ministerial delays and diversions, if carefully and faithfully managed need not prove to become ministerial abortion or abandonment!

Please follow with me and let's together navigate Apostle Paul's "crises points" that would eventually turn out to be remarkable turning points in his ministry.

## Apostle Paul's Crises & Turning Points

## # 1. The Antioch Church's Crises

*A. Mark's Abandonment of Paul in Perga-Pamphylia:*
Persecution had broken out in the Jerusalem Church. Stephen's eventual death in *Acts 7* was one major consequence of the earliest persecution; the entire membership of the Church – excluding the apostles – had been scattered throughout the regions of Judea and Samaria (Acts 8:1).

A severe famine which was recorded as *"throughout all the world"* struck in the days of Claudius Caesar.[8] Closely following this natural disaster was King Herod's persecution and eventual execution of James the twin brother of John the Beloved.[9] Next, Apostle Peter was apprehended in *Acts 12* but was dramatically saved through the mighty deliverance of God's Angel! Survivors of the harsh blows dealt the Church had gone *underground*; they were intensely praying in Mrs. Mary Mark's house. This was where Peter had resorted to immediately he had recovered from the shock of Heaven's angelic rescue from an untimely death![10]

Now, Mrs. Mary Mark was a sibling of Barnabas – and the mother of John Mark, a disciple Paul and Barnabas had brought with them away from the *hurricane* of Jerusalem onto Antioch, solely to serve as their *'minister.'*[11]

Today, almost everyone who perceives of some measure of anointing upon their lives wants to be in the limelight, ministering from the pulpit. Followers of unspiritual leaders also have not made this concept, easier to understand, by *any* means! But the way we refer to ministers in christian ministries today was *not* the original intended root meaning of John Mark's specified role of duties. Rather to the contrary, Mark's life was meant to be *'poured out'* unreservedly to God's service under Barnabas and Paul. Mark was meant to have waited on them; much like an Orient slave had *ministered* to – or waited upon – his owner or master. Or the waiters at Marks & Spencer's or any other *posh* joint/eatery had waited on your *very* self at a table, as you had ordered your courses! John Mark was to be a servant of Paul – even as Paul was a servant of God!

But all of a sudden, John Mark would opt out! We really would not be so specifically certain as to what went wrong in their relationships that had made him abruptly abdicate his *ministry* to Paul. Whatever it was, we know the separation was necessitated by an urgent need that *had* arisen in Mrs. Mark's household! It was not planned that Mark would abscond forever, though. Bible Scholars have speculated that the effects of the great "world-wide" famine was hard hitting upon Mrs. Mary Mark in Jerusalem – among many other inhabitants – and John's attention had been urgently requested. She had needed him to lend a saving hand to prevent her from taking a seeming inevitable financial plunge.

Family ministries are great! But a great deal of caution needed being exercised with restraints firmly anchored, so that fraternal accords do *not* estrange spiritual bonding! This could lead to great misunderstandings in family-ministries, or blended-marriages. The crisis here is totally, an issue of loyalty! You have seen it very plainly, how John Mark's *disloyalty* almost undermined Paul's ministry!

Because of the intricate patterns of family-ministries and the emotions often associated with them (for those whose families are concerned) and the seeming un-emotionalism or dis-enfranchisement that could be involved (on the part of people like Paul who have no children or spouses); Paul could not readily reconcile Mark's decision to abandon *his* call for family!

At a later date, when the apostle and Barnabas deliberated upon who was to travel with them on their second missionary journey, Barnabas had wanted his nephew on the team, but Paul had declined his request. That was it: the contention between them being *"so sharp"*, they parted asunder one from the other.[12]

We would however never again hear of Barnabas' evangelistic thrusts. He never sailed past Cyprus; their first outreach milepost! Such is the price you seem to choose to pay for being emotionally tied to your relations though you really have been genuinely called into the ministry, marriage – or other 'life or death' ventures.

Take the Lord's warning to heart:

> *"If any man come to me, and hate not his father, and mother, and wife, and children, and brethren, and sisters, yea, and his own life also, he cannot be my disciple."*
> Luke 14:26

After a few more years of spiritual maturity though, John Mark would submissively return and re-apply for re-absorption into St. Paul's team.

*Would you have considered re-admitting Mark onto your team?*

The great apostle definitely was very much unlike me; he had granted and re-accepted John Mark's request! Paul's magnanimous action was an awesome, amazing demonstration of an incomprehensible grace and maturity in leadership. I am taking my cues already!

## B. Infiltrations of Heretical Teachers into the Body:

On one hand, none other factor as persecution rouses and awakens a sleeping church to her tasks. Persecution, most often in the end often genders unto a healthy growth! On the other hand, none other factor dares threaten to collapse a strong, virile being as internal bleeding caused by a cancerous growth: my assertion also holds true for animate beings!

From the handy accounts presented us by Dr. Luke in *Acts11:19-21*, the church in Antioch had been an offshoot of the seed of the persecution and the execution of Stephen. Now, *her* total existence was strongly threatened by the hot steam exhaled by this *giant of the tribe of heretical teachings:*

> *"And certain men which came down from Judea taught the brethren, and said except ye be circumcised after the manner of Moses, ye cannot be saved."*
> Acts 15:1

We know that God specifically commissioned Paul as *the* evangelist and apostle to the Gentile world; the other apostles should focus upon the Jews and their *trado-religious* sentiments. That, however, was not Paul's thing![13]

In these days of an increase in false prophets performing lying wonders, deceiving and deluding countless multitudes and thus making strong encroachment attempts to infiltrate and deceive the very elect, the Body of Christ must be vigilant. True servants of God must unanimously rise up to expose, confront and condemn the hidden works of darkness. These are no days to play *ping-pong* with *"the unclean spirits like frogs that came out of the mouths of the dragon ... the beast ... and the false prophet."*[14]

Believers in Christ must be willing to rise equivocally to petition our governments to not promulgate and pass into laws, legislations inspired by *the unclean spirits like frogs that came out of the mouth of the dragon!*

> *"For they are the spirits of the devils, working miracles, which go forth unto the kings of the earth and of the whole world, to gather them to the battle of that great day of God Almighty."*
> Revelation 16:14

It wouldn't be Paul alone who would confront the heretics. The spiritual principle of unity of purpose, voice, act and will – more than often times – has guaranteed resounding victory against this pack of hell's hounds.

> *"When therefore Paul and Barnabas had no small dissension and disputation with them, they determined that Paul and Barnabas, and certain other of them, should go up to Jerusalem unto the apostles and elders about this question."*
> Acts 15:2

Fortunately for the Antioch church, the news of their struggle against these demonic agents of discord reached the Jerusalem Church's *Council of Elders* with the quickest alacrity. Their reaction was a unilateral condemnation of the subversive elements:

> *"For as much as we have heard, that certain which went out from us have troubled you with words, subverting your souls, saying, Ye must be circumcised, and keep the law: to whom we gave no such commandment."*

In this age of globalized technological interactivity, we must take advantage of the technological advancement as wings upon which to spread the Gospel. That way, we would 'break the devil's back' quickest, being able to interconnect, share information, and proffer solutions to issues of urgent concerns! The Antioch church – obviously in distress *had* to find the quickest, surest mode of how the news of their impending crisis would reach the Headquarters, in Jerusalem:

> *"And being brought on their way by the church, they passed through Phenice and Samaria ..."*
> Acts 15:3

## 8 Turning Points in Antioch Church's Crisis

The following are some of the blessings yielded the Apostle and his team through the instrumentality of the Antioch church's crises:

• *First, the Validation of Paul's Ministry:*
Paul's ministry's validation to the Gentile world – and the Constitution for achieving this feat were unanimously agreed upon and released by the other apostles and elders in the Jerusalem headquarter church:

> *"For it seemed good to the Holy Ghost, and to us, to lay upon you no greater burden than these necessary things;*
>
> *That ye abstain from meats offered to idols, and from blood, and from things strangled, and from fornication: from which if ye keep yourselves, ye shall do well. Fare ye well."*
> Acts 15:28-29

We understand that after they had journeyed to Antioch and had eventually *"delivered the epistle,"* reading it in the hearing of the multitude; the whole church *"rejoiced for the consolation"* of it.[15]

Every christian ministry requires God's authenticity; but also man's, so that they would not have run in vain! The qualified person to authenticate your ministry would be your mentor – and the ministry relations you have maintained over the years.[16] No, God would *not* alone endorse your ministry; He always had undertaken this task *side by side* the elders, your fore-runners. Remember, Jesus' ministry's validation had been granted by the Holy Spirit in the River Jordan accompanied by the *"voice of one crying in the wilderness,"* even John the Baptist, His fore-runner.[17]

*Have you a fore-runner?*

Paul had his fore-runners in *"James, Cephas, and John, who seemed to be pillars"* in the Jerusalem church.[18]

- *Second, the Sudden Availability of Church's Statement of Faith/Constitution:*

The pursuance of a statement of faith enshrined in the early Church's constitution had led to the spiritual establishment of converts – and a numerical increase in the young church! Same occurrence had been recorded at Lystra and Iconium in *Acts 16:4-5*:

> *"And as they went through the cities, they delivered them the decrees for to keep, that were ordained of the apostles and elders which were at Jerusalem.*

And so were the churches established in the faith, and increased in number daily."

• *Third, the Opening of a Ministerial Accountability opportunity:*
Opportunity was availed Paul and Barnabas to render a comprehensive *"First Missionary Journey's Report"* of *"miracles and wonders God had wrought among the Gentiles by them"* to the high-power Jerusalem Council.[19]

• *Fourth, Untold favors Bestowed upon Paul's ministry:*
Because of their convincing testimonies shared above, untold favors attended Paul and his team – beginning from the Jerusalem plaza:

> *"Then pleased it the apostles and elders, with the whole church ..."*
>
> Acts 15:22

• *Fifth, Delegated Manpower Exchange:*
A re-engineered spiritually and technically-fit exchange of delegated manpower resulted between the parent and satellite churches. We were informed that *"chosen men of their own company"* were sent to Antioch with Paul and Barnabas:

> *"Then pleased it the apostles and elders, with the whole church, to send chosen men of their own company to Antioch with Paul and Barnabas: namely, Judas surnamed, Barsabas, and Silas, chief men among the brethren."*
>
> Acts 15:22

Not only were delegated team members spiritually and technically fit, we were further informed of Barsabas' and Silas' wholeheartedness with respect to Kingdom service. Much like Caleb and Joshua, Barsabas and Silas were: *"Men that have hazarded their lives for the name of our Lord Jesus Christ."*[20]

- *Sixth, A formal Recognition of the Antioch church:*
A formal recognition of the Antioch church by the Jerusalem church took place, an occasion which resulted into a spiritual bonding that would eventually necessitate the apostolic visit – at a later date – of the ageing Apostle Peter and his entourage to such a place as far away as Antioch.[21]

- *Seventh, God remembered to Honor the 'faithful':*
Long time 'faithful' such as the Cypriot Joe Barsabas Justus – *"the son of encouragement"* – would find his services requested by the strong, influential delegation sent to strengthen the distressed Antioch church.[22] You would recall that same Barsabas had earlier in church history contested to fill Judas Iscariot's vacant apostleship – and had lost.[23] He had lost that lofty post to Matthias; yet he had not been discouraged, neither had his enthusiasm dipped. Rather, he had faithfully kept up with the worship and service at whatever level the opportunity had availed itself! Many years later, the faithful God would request his services as a missionary to the church in Antioch. *What an inspiring lesson for some position-drunk, vision-impaired, mission-lost, politics-ridden workers of today's successful mega-churches!*

- *Eighth, An International Ministry Opportunity opened unto Silas:*
Silas, a *'localized'* inhabitant of Jerusalem who had caught a burden for the troubled Antioch church – as well as Paul's ministry, after ministering there for a while – would be invited aboard by Apostle Paul as a worthy companion in replacement of Barnabas.[24]

The rationale behind Silas' acute resolve to remain in Antioch ought to rest the bones missionaries pick in ascertaining whether it is the call that justifies the need or the need that justifies the call!

Thus were the Antioch Church's crises overcome by the erstwhile Apostle Paul. A little later though, he should gear up for yet another crisis!

# # 2. Paul's Ministerial Diversion Crisis: The Macedonian 'SOS' Call

The apostle's first missionary journey was a tremendous success: the word of the Lord had taken roots in the peoples' hearts – and some churches had been planted! Demolishing *the giant of heretics' heresies* – in Antioch, for instance – would only accentuate the expediency of Paul and his team to visit again all the overseas churches planted through their efforts. This was how their second missionary journey was conceived:

> *"And some days after Paul said unto Barnabas, Let us go again and visit our brethren in every city where we have preached the word of the Lord, and see how they do."*
>
> Acts 15:36

Missionary journeys do *not* come cheap: the many hours that have been invested into praying, planning and preparation by God's ministers are enormous. These are the necessary spiritual costs.[25]

*What of the equally important financial costs; who bears such heavy financial outlays?*

Necessarily, the parent church in Jerusalem – would be the sending church. But the overseas churches also needed to share in the commitments that are requested of them in abiding by the ministry's *Statement of Faith,* as encapsulated in the newly released constitution!

The response of these younger churches to the organizational re-structure appended by the Jerusalem church was overwhelming. We read in *Acts 16:4-5* that:

> "*As they went through the cities, they delivered them the decrees for to keep, that were ordained of the apostles and elders which were at Jerusalem.*
>
> *And so were the churches established in the faith, and increased in number daily.*"

Evidently, we see four outstanding, *'must have'* ingredients that must be embedded in the success equation of the headship of a new or growing ministry, vis-à-vis:

- *vision;*
- *zeal to advance the kingdom work;*
- *pre-conception of their destination; (translating they had accurate direction and focus); and,*
- *possession of the means for going - the Antioch church would defray the apostle's team's initial landing costs and sundry expenses.*

Apart from the local church raising funds generally, individuals *"whose hearts the Lord touched,"* became partners of the ministry! (Acts 16:14-15)

## *Divine Timing in Callings*

The Lord of the harvest awaited the approaching footfalls of His dear laborers as they endeavored to advance the

Gospel to wider Asia. He would re-direct both their steps and re-order their elaborate schedules!

Whenever God punctuates a calling, ministry or an outreach, it is because He is about to re-direct the course of events for a greater yield! God's calling is without repentance; hence, He never permits a delay in purpose for no just cause(s). Our duty it is to seek His face so as to receive fresh directives from Him.

We are engaged in a constant battle with the forces of hell; battle which our Master Jesus had already guaranteed us winning, because He'd fought and won. There is no question about that. Our concern, hence, ought to be that we arm ourselves with such understanding that Generals are *not* made *'boot-polishing and brass-licking'* in the barracks, rather; God's Generals earn their brass after having been exposed to fierce warfare. This was Paul's fate – and that of his team-mates:

> "Now when they had gone throughout Phrygia and the region of Galatia, and were forbidden of the Holy Ghost to preach the word in Asia."
>
> Acts 16:6

Kindly read again, above verses more solemnly.

*What did you read?*

MISSION TO ASIA SUSPENDED!

*Now,* put yourself in Paul's position.

*Could you anticipate your emotions? And probably those of your team-mates?*

You should *not* lack noticing a few attitudes flying off their handles, if you are observant and keen! I could imagine myself a little discouraged, now. In my discouragement, with a tone that never would have lacked a gruffly accent, I would have summoned the Lord: *"What have I done wrong, Lord? Could it be that I'd added a wrong person as Jonah on my team lately? Maybe the whole planning was wrong ..."*

If you were like me, you would manufacture a thousand "maybe's" in a jiffy!

I would demand of my lieutenant, Silas: *"Hey! What's the matter, Silas? Couldn't we reach Bithynia through Mysia? There ought to be a way out: you're a prophet, aren't you?"*

Please be honest with yourself: anyone could have become troubled!

The scripture revealed Paul's natural reaction: he ordered his team to advance! *Did you ever notice that?* For we read:

> *"After they were come to Mysia, they assayed to go into Bithynia: but the Spirit suffered them."*
>
> Acts16:7

Who 'suffered' – prevented – them from advancing into Bithynia?

The Holy Spirit of God!

In the Apostle's record of leading and commandeering outreaches and Gospel expeditions, this would be two misses in a row. Two barricaded attempts; two 'blocked' entrances! Barricades, blockages and delays can cause frustrations, deep anguish and evoke feelings of rejection and/or resentment.

*Have you experienced a blockage or a barricade in ministry, business or family life recently – and thus was about to quit in anger, frustration or hurt?* Listen, God has *not* rejected nor forgotten you. Instead, He has a better opportunity awaiting your assault.

*Your* reaction to *barricades* or *restraints* is the giant *you* would need to be aware of at this time. Your battle format would be to closely monitor the thoughts of your heart, the utterances of your mouth and the comportment of your frame. One great attribute you must be more than willing to imbibe is the stealth nature of the hunting tiger: he prowls slowly but steadily towards his target, focus – locked onto it!

*A deep understanding to inculcate in yourself is a firm assurance that if a door closes; a bigger, wider, better door will swing open of its accord if you dare bend towards the opposite of that which was firmly shut.* This is winning wisdom over the giant of blockages, barricades and restraints! Apostle Paul would "pass by" the closed door – bypass moaning, frustrations and discouragements; and instead, proceed towards Troas:

"*And they passing by Mysia came down to Troas.*"
Acts 16:8

'*What geographical locations are your Asia, Mysia and Bithynia? What/Who is it that you are holding onto so tightly that you wouldn't let go, after the door has been firmly shut? What girl, for instance, are you still pursuing when she has told you certainly that she has foreclosed on your repeated offers?*'

Hear me soundly, please: it is in *your* demonstrated flexibility to positively "pass by Mysia"; to stretch towards a feel for a 'further' reach, that births angelic manifestations!

Subsequent to their arriving Troas – and before they would *till the ground*, God would certify the obedient apostle and his team victorious, in wrestling with this giant; intervene and re-direct their footsteps. Hence the super-natural occurred:

> *"And a vision appeared to Paul in the night; there stood a man of Macedonia, and prayed him, saying, Come over into Macedonia, and help us.*
>
> *And after he had seen the vision, immediately we endeavoured to go into Macedonia, assuredly gathering that the Lord had called us for to preach the gospel unto them."*
> Acts 16:9-10

Though *war fronts* are *battle fronts*, yet they are the only zones acknowledged by Heaven for the recovery (and discovery) of spoils/gems! God would re-direct His servants to Philippi, a town and a people that would prove essential and beneficial to their missionary exploits in years to come.

At this juncture, shall I share with you some signs that should confirm God's re-directing a destiny, ministry or business?

## *Signs of God's Re-Direction*

- *"How would I know God is re-directing me?"*

- *"How would I know for certain that God really wants us to move house, shop, office ...?"*

- *"How would I know for sure God wants me to end this relationship, courtship or engagement?*

If these are some of the questions agitating your mind, my prayer is that you overcome such confusion – and the associated pains, in Christ's name. Remember, *"God is not the author of confusion."*[26]

These major signs, therefore, derived from Acts 16:6-12 are evident pointers to God's re-direction/closed door:

i. *When the Holy Spirit restrains, forbids, restricts or disallows:*

> *"After they were come to Mysia, they assayed to go into Bithynia, but the Spirit suffered them not."*
> Verse 7

*How does the Spirit of God restrain, forbid, restrict or disallow the execution of a project or the performance of a thing?*

The simplest answer to this question is that He withdraws His power from that particular project. Or He restrains His *very self!* Contrary to popular impression, God's Holy Spirit *never* does withdraw His presence away from a sealed child of God.

The keyword is *'sealed'*, taken from Ephesians 4:30:

> *"And grieve not the Holy Spirit of God, whereby ye are sealed unto the day of redemption."*

This specifically means that the Holy Spirit could be grieved, and thus restrained. In the alternative, He could *'rope us up'* - and we become restrained!

Therefore, *if* the Holy Spirit forbids, you:

a.) *would hear the whisper of His "still small voice"* – that is, the inner witness, attesting the fact that you are engaged in a wrong timing of the execution of an assignment;

*b.) may feel an almost indescribable strange impression upon your spirit-man's emotions.* A decision soon to be taken which ought to have caused an excitement causes trepidation or a flat taste;

*c.) could experience a general restlessness in your spirit-man*, but you must be sensitive in order for that to happen, and/or;

*d.) would experience series of closed doors like Paul and his team-mates.*

Closed door means, for example, one *endeavoring to go* but is *restrained from going*. Signs and wonders, usual exhibitions in ministrations and a normal lifestyle suddenly drastically reduce or completely disappear. Series of hardships could also ensue.

*ii.) When we experience "a toil-for-naught-all-night":*
Peter held onto being a hardworking fish-businessman on the Lake of Gennesaret when the Savior would indeed have him become a skilled successful fisher of men's lost souls. He and his fishermen crew toiled all night – and caught nothing!

Frustrated and angry, they were washing their nets. Then the Master called onto them to *"return to business,"* albeit temporarily – so He could demonstrate to the *eyes of their minds, a* new calling!

He asked them to *"launch out and let down their nets "for a haul."* And a haul, they indeed caught, so much so that they requested their partners and their boats to come to their rescue before they started sinking. Master Jesus had performed a miracle past their intellectual expectations. Peter needed no more conviction of his sin of holding out against the Lord's call upon his life.[27] When they had managed to bring their boats and fishes ashore, *"they forsook all, and followed"* Jesus![28]

*iii.) When financial conduit pipes are either blocked or damaged thus rendering for instance, ordinary basic existence, most difficult or totally unbearable.* Debt incurring may also be on the toll!

*iv.) When your insensitivity or callousness to the Spirit endures, your stubbornness would be rewarded with angelic oppositions – instead of ministrations – as had been Balaam's experience in Numbers 22:26-31.*

*v.) When the situation in ' iv' persists, it could lead to a stiff penalty being paid by the christian as evident in Jonah's experience.* A whale would swallow him up for three days and nights; pour gastric juice all over him, before thinking it a done deal to vomit him onto the shores of Nineveh. When the prophet had been *re-produced,* he had been *re-packaged!* His variegated appearance alone was more than enough convicting message to the sinful megacity of Nineveh to repent – and turn toward God!

## *Mandatory Expected Reactions of a Child of God to the Spirit's Re-Direction*

Once you have begun to experience *any* of the conditions described above, it could be the Lord is bidding you a re-direction in *your* course! Your re-actions, favorable, to the Spirit's bidding, will ensure the certainty of your arrival at your destination with un-imaginable blessings.

Some of the expected favorable reactions of a sensitive child of God to His re-directions include:

*i.) Calmness:*
Do *not* forge ahead in heavy fog! Pause and be calm. Frankly, this is one of such periods you mandatorily must *"be still and know that (He is) God – and that He is with you!"*[29]

*ii.) More frequent fellowship with the Word of God:*
You must carve out and crave for more time of fellowship with God through the reading and studying of the Bible, His word. This divine act was exemplified by David during one of his lifetime's most tormenting experiences; he'd pursued his enemies, overtaken, and recovered all the Amalekites had raided![30] You too will recover all if you follow these simple suggestions.

*iii.) Watchings, fortified with fastings and prayerfulness among other activities listed, for example, in 2 Corinthians11:27.*

*iv.) Sensitivity in the Spirit.*

*v.) Spontaneity of action; that is, immediacy, obeying a new order, a new word of instruction or a new vision:*
Do not rationalize the new directive. Launch out at once!

> *"And after he had seen the vision, immediately we endeavoured to go into Macedonia ..."*
>
> Acts 16:10

*vi.) Joyfully embracing the fresh directives issued by God:*
Doctor Luke recounts that immediately God had spoken to Paul: *"... we endeavoured to go ..."*

Do not accept the new challenge with your *mental person* while your *spirit-person* is hesitant. That could prove fatal.

*vii.) Multi-lateral acceptance, when a team is involved:*
Paul was *the* Team leader. He saw the *new* vision. He communicated the vision understandably well to his team mates. On their part, Luke reported that they ALL *"assuredly gathered"* this was the Holy Spirit's new course

for their destiny; and for the larger part, in the destiny of the Christian enterprise.

Notice, God never breaks protocols. He always communicates the directions or re-directions to the *Paul's* and *not* the whole Team; to the *Moses'*, not the *Aaron's* and *Miriam's!* Now, if the *head* receives the instructions, it follows then, that the *body parts* need not being coaxed into following in the spirit of godly obedience! Beware of the spirit of rancor within the camp; it will *not* let you inherit your promised land!

# # 3. The Macedonian Town Crisis

Man's bumper harvest of God's faithfulness is not often always reaped in the short run. After *"assuredly gathering"* the Lord would have them invade Macedonia with the Gospel, it would be most unthinkable to visualize what troubles and misfortunes would soon befall them. After more than two decades of success on the job, Paul had developed a winning strategy of *storming the city where the action was!* So Philippi, a colony, a melting pot and a seaside town which was the second largest city in the Roman province of Macedonia was targeted.

From this *action city*, Paul believed the Gospel flame would be fanned into an explosive fireball, large enough to consume the then whole world, in its billowy flames.

Obviously, Thessalonica, the largest and the capital city of the same province would next most likely draw Paul and Team's spiritual archery skills.

Furthermore, Philippi was considered above other cities because Paul's ship had berthed on the shores of this town entering from Neapolis; Thessalonica, much father away. Logistical planning must be weighed with extreme thoughtfulness, consideration and spiritual alertness. Philippi, already marked out on the *Drawing Board* would become the Team's beachhead for *"certain days"* according to the account in *Acts16:12*.

Spiritual war generals of the Lord of Hosts are not the only ones that strategize on Drawing Boards; the devil and his hosts also do! So the devil also had identified and earmarked the apostle's beach-head for a *principality* crisis!

## Paul's Rendezvous with a Demonic, Remote-controlled Fortune-Teller

The following highlights show Paul's crises-points in Philippi *viz – a – viz* a rendezvous with a principality-controlled fortune teller young lady. Dr. Luke recorded:

> *"And it came to pass, as we went to prayer, a certain damsel possessed with a spirit of divination met us, which brought her masters much gain by soothsaying."*
> 
> Acts16:16

But she was hell's ambush!

Let me show you how to avoid hell's ambush:

*i.) Avoid unhealthy spiritual attachment(s):*
The devil knew that both the team and its leader were *'sold out'* both to the Lord – and the Lord of the harvest. Satan knew Paul and his team would require human contacts and partners that would make the task of planting the new church in Philippi much easier to accomplish. So acting

the first page of his scripts, Satan commandeered the principality of Macedonia; this *'medium lady'* to *tail* Paul and the team!

Luke's eye-witness account included this weighty sentence:

> *"The same followed Paul and us."*
> Acts16:17

In other words, this principality-controlled lady had aligned and latched herself onto the *Paul Outreach Team*. And very soon, at first, God's General noticed how 'gifted' she was: *she could prophesy, oh my!*

Let me sound you a note of caution: beware of unhealthy spiritual, soulish (emotional) and physical ties! Some of your new associations may have been agents on assignment, planted on you by the pit of hell, to ensnare and lay ambushes for you.

Be alert. Watch for revealing signs; prayerfully approach *any* alliance(s).

*ii.) Be wary of any who praise-sings people/God's servants:*

> *"The same followed Paul and us, and cried, saying, These men are the servants of the most high God, which shew unto us the way of salvation.*
>
> *And this did she many days ..."*
> Acts16:17-18a

Her *modus operandi* was this kind of slow poison prowess only found in snake-bites. But the *Standby*, the Holy Spirit, would restrain His listening servant from sliding down the wheels of Satan's deceptive machinations where he would have been mercilessly crushed.

*How would the Holy Spirit accomplish this task of notifying Paul of the fake I.D of this supposed 'lady prophetess'?*

We noted earlier that the Spirit would communicate His grievance *'pricking'* Paul's Spirit. The Bible says: *"But by sorrow of the heart, the (human) spirit is broken," (Proverbs15:13 emphasis, mine).* Furthermore, we read of the Holy Spirit's act of warning unto the apostle:

*"But Paul being grieved ..."*
Acts16:18

That word *'grieved'* as used in this context, in the original tongue has been used to describe a tree *"being hewn down."* In essence, the Holy Spirit ensured Paul's spirit was *"hewed down."*

Let me quip here, that a super-sensitive servant of the Lord must *not* only *watch the lips of the Spirit*; he must be well tutored to *watch the emotions* of the Spirit. The Holy Spirit displays a variety of emotions. He may *not* always talk. Paul got the Spirit's feeling when his spirit had being grieved!

*iii.) Beware when a person lays a repetitive pressure, unduly:*
Laying repetitive pressure on a person to do a thing, conform to an order or make a decision is a clear manifestation of the spirit of manipulation to seek control of that person. Simply, it is witchcraft! That was the serpent's same method at "beguiling" Eve in the Garden of Eden; Portiphar's wife's trickery on holy Joseph – and now this false prophetess', on Paul!

*iv.) Spare not; Cast out the demonic spirit – but not dissociate:*
Paul cast out the principality of Philippi: *"But Paul being grieved turned and said to the Spirit, I command thee in the name of Jesus Christ to come out of her. And he came out the same hour"* (Acts 16:18). Paul's casting out of the profiting divination principality of Philippi meant an immediate sack of the lady's masters!

## Effects on the Apostolic Team & the City of Philippi On the Occasion of Unseating Philippi's Principal Demon

You see, when the church is filled with brave, sensitive, Holy Spirit-filled servants of God, she should soon vaporize the false prophets' securities – and ransom the elect. Unseating the principal demon of Philippi would elucidate some rippling effects on the apostolic team as well as the city itself. Here, shared below, are some of those effects on Paul and his team:

*i.) They were seriously maligned and assaulted before the magistrates, (verse 19);*

*ii.) They were misinformed upon and thus suffered racist attacks for being Jews, (verses 20&21):*
Fortunately, Paul and Silas – among the team – each possessed dual-citizenship! They were not only Jewish but fully Romans!

*iii.) Their bodies were broken by many stripes (verse 22), and finally;*

*iv.) Having broken their bodies, the devil proceeded at a ploy to break their spirit. They were "hogged" into a Maximum Security Prison without a fair trial (verses 23&24).*

Whenever you witness anyone who faces a barrage of attacks of this magnitude, you must realize that they are being attacked by one of hell's *giants!* If they overcame this ruthless opposition from hell – and they sure did, Paul and Silas should rejoice because they are *en route* possessing Philippi for the King of kings and the Lord of lords; and not only Philippi, but the entire civilized Europe!

## *Emerging Blessings from the Macedonian Crisis*

Part of the effects on Paul's ministry of engaging in this spiritual conflict – and overcoming were the blessings that emerged from the crisis in Philippi. Here are the sweet blessings, succinctly shared:

*i.) A vibrant church was planted:*
The Philippian church was the first church planted by the apostle on European soil. By contrast, the team had earlier felt led to go into Asia but the Spirit had suffered them – and had instead re-directed them to Europe.

*Are you currently experiencing a re-direction of God's Spirit in your life? You may have started out headed for the East; yet He bids you: "Turn left, left; to the West!"*

*ii.) Influential people received the Goodnews:*
A few influential people came to the knowledge of the Lord Jesus Christ. These are the crème-de-la-crème of the megacity of Philippi. These – and their loved ones – formed

the bedrock of the young church. Ponder for a minute or two, on a young church's *Baptismal Register* which included names as:

- the Asiatic Jewess merchant Lydia, *"the seller of purple"* and all of her household; contacts/friends whom the apostle had met at the beach side as reported in *Acts 16:13*;
- the gifted, healed and delivered beautiful Greek slave lady formerly manipulated by the fortune telling spirit *(Acts16:16-18)*;
- the top civil servant Roman jailor – and his entire household who had subsequently been converted after they had witnessed the earthquake of deliverance of God's servants, and;
- notable rich converts of Paul's first missionary trip such as Roman Governor Sergius Paulus who could because of Philippi's vantage sea-front location, speed-sail his speedboat or yacht to the Philippian church's Sunday and weekly services.

*iii.) The Philippian church grew to become the most supportive – when all others stopped supporting the apostle's ministry:*

At least, four different times had the Philippians magnanimously financially supported their apostle's ministry. Blessed is any apostle who successfully underwent crises that eventually qualified him to have as a home church, the sweetness of the Philippians!

Even in the latter years of the aged apostle's house arrest in Rome, this church never for once failed to send their moral, financial and spiritual support.

The only threatening, limiting factor in a church exhibiting such status, culture and opulence as the Philippians' was an undercutting current such as the personality clash recorded between the two sisters Euodias and Syntyche.[30]

iv.) *Philippi's status as a thriving seaport as well as Europe's melting pot provided Apostle Paul's gospel message with eagle wings with which to soar into the civilized world of European and Greek scholarly thoughts.*

v.) *St. Paul and his team were accorded their rightful respect:*
After their public humiliation and imprisonment without trial, Paul's and Silas' Roman I.D's were soon publicly declared unto the Magistrates. Radically, the respect and rights of passage they had been entitled to – but which had been denied, were quickly restored unto and accorded them respectively![31]

vi.) *The principality of Philippi had been dethroned; the bewitching of souls and fortune-telling through the spirit of divination had been dethroned:*
As demonic principalities over geo-political landscapes – and strongholds in peoples' minds – are responsible for a wide range of un-wholesome evil behavioral patterns such as fortune-telling, bewitchment, witchcraft, sorcery, divorcement, violence, gruesome murders, rape, incest – and other associated evils; Philippi's notoriety and image had suddenly began to assume a rotund, more favorable expression in testament to the power of God to set men free.

vii.) *The advent of Apostle Paul's second missionary journey through the cities of Derbe and Lystra birthed a viable spiritual son, Timothy:*
The synoptic account of Timothy's background is

chronicled in *Acts 16:1-3*. Young Timothy was a handsome teenager of mixed parentage: mother being Jewish and father, an un-named Greek.[32] The inclusion of half-Gentile Timothy on Paul's team-list would soon bolster the Apostle's ministry efforts to the Gentile world. Timothy would also later become the youngest Bishop of the Church at Ephesus in his late teens!

## My prayer for you

As we come to a close of the Macedonian crisis and its inherent turning points, I earnestly pray over you:

*"May the Lord take you through the crisis designed to form the right character within you, so that you may be divinely equipped to deal with the blessings that are ear-marked for you!*

*May you also experience such awesome in-filling and an outpouring of the Holy Spirit that would enable you conquer your giants in Jesus' mighty name, Amen!*

*Chapter 7*

# How to Maximally Profit in Delay

*"Everything comes to those who hustle while they wait."*
                              *- Thomas A. Edison*

I must have been five or six; or thereabout.

It was threatening to rain that mid-morning in August. The winds never blew ever so hard, a little robin had been caught off guard. She had veered off course into our living room.

Our first family house was situated in a 'middle class', developing suburb of the '50's; South West of Ibadan, Nigeria. It was a beautiful bungalow with collapsible, double-leaved wooden panels that served as windows. Atop each pair of *'flap – windows'* sat a small, rectangular plain glass window called "lattice-window," or a "far-light piece." It was through one partly opened *'far-light piece'* that the boisterous wind had navigated the wet robin into the strange land.

I was excited as I watched the confused and agitated little creature hop from place to place in that confined space. Frightened by the unfamiliar surroundings and this *giant* statue watching her, the distressed little robin chirped and frantically fluttered her wings – hurling itself against the *far-lights* in the process of anticipating its escape. It had slowly but agreeably dawned upon her that this was going to be a confinement.

I had watched long enough! In my little mind must have raced more than a thousand thoughts about the bird's eventual fate.

*"I would invite my friends in to come and adore my August visitor,"* I had summed up.

Exhausted and resigned to fate; her perfect glassy eyes and beaks wide opened, the tired little robin eventually perched on a burglar-proof rod, expectant of help!

Carefully, I reached for the trembling creature, stroked her body, and adored her small cute features before passing her along in between the exchanges of other four little pairs of hands and warm glow of glimpses.

Little robin was finally handed over to me to determine her fate as she was *'my bird.'*

One of my little hands 'cupped' the stunned little creature. The other climbed a wooden stool! I partly undid the window latch – and consequently released the bewildered bird, off into her destiny!

It flew off happily, chirping along as on and on it flew!

Even though this incident occurred almost four decades ago, I know that this could be somebody's story today; it will help shed a major beam of light on what our actions should be if we suffer *any* delay!

## What to Do when Delayed?

*i.) Come to a Place of Rest:*
First and foremost, my little robin came to a place of rest. It stopped fluttering her wings, hopping from place to place anticipating a quick escape! So must you, too. Whenever you are confronted with and rattled by issues surrounding the *mid-life crisis*; instead of reacting *up-beat* to the heat of the battle, please learn to be calm and patient.

Wait – and possibly do nothing until the clouds of confusion, guilt and anger, bitterness and depression billow over, no matter how long it may take.

But *we* are creatures that love to hurry – and worry! The fibers in our whole entity – body, soul and spirit – *will* react to delay! We may be *pressured* to do something; as this is the whole essence of temptation!

*ii.) In temptations, Be patient:*
A temptation is defined as pressure applied to our senses to think, say or do wrong; hence performing below expectation or *par*!

Being calm in the midst of trouble is "irrational" to our modern thought process, isn't it? But you know what the Bible says to us to do *with* temptation, don't you? We are *not* told to consider, contemplate, analyze or reason out a temptation! God's Word asks us to endure *the* temptation!

The *Amplifies Version* of the Bible says: *"Blessed is the man who is patient under trial and stands up under temptation, for when he has stood the test, and been approved, he will receive {the victor's} crown of life which God has promised to those who love Him"* (James 1:12).

You are *not* to buckle under the strain of temptation, but rather be patient and bear *the* burden, *the* shame, *the* pressure, and *the* lure. Your ability to do this is one of the hallmarks of a sweet, matured christian spirit; the ability to be *patient in tribulation*.

The closest people to you are the instruments the devil will hi-jack and use against you in your desperate moments. He will use them to proffer solutions that are worldly to your spiritual issues. Therefore when friends, families and loved ones bear down the pressure *on* you – and express their concerned feelings for and proffer solutions to you on issues that trouble you; for instance, *'why you haven't yet gotten married at thirty, or not had your own children being married for ten years, or not attained that particular rank or title?'* you know what to do: b-e-a-r *the* pressure, patiently! Don't chicken out or compromise. Neither let your changing emotions betray your faith!

I am not advocating emotional suppression; what I am saying is that you must effectively curtail your emotions and not let them outburst or control you!

*iii.) Compose your demeanor, Contain your spirit:*
Not only must you contain your emotions, you must both compose your demeanor, self-portrait and looks – along with a well controlled mouth. Do not speak *"un-advisedly with your lips"* as did an angry Moses, at a crucial point in

his career!¹ That happened to be his costliest mistake, for he never possessed Canaan.

*Have you noticed that waiting is the hardest – yet, most rewarding task ever known to humanity?* Neither also has yet been found as efficient a tool to be deployed as silence, when compassed by the giants of envy, jealousy and wrath – or enemies that have laid watch for your words!

Dogged by a stiff, sweat-producing chase by troubled king Saul, God ordered David: *"Be still and know that I am God."*²

The root word here is *'still.'* In the original tongue, the word *'still'* connotes a negative meaning of *"slackness"*; which if applied in the spiritual, turns into an avalanche of strength. It could further imply: *"abate"*, *"cease"*, *"wax feeble"*, *"let alone"* and *"become weak."*

In essence, irrespective of the protracted delay you have experienced, God is saying: *"You be calm, I am in control!"* Rendered in today's everyday English you would have heard God say: *"You be cool, calm and collected; I'm still the Boss; I'm still in charge. So, relax!"*

Leading psychologists have cautioned that we can deplete much quicker, our physical and mental strengths reserved for a week's job by "boiling over" an issue just for an hour! Cases of exhaustion and actual collapse have been recorded for the reason of uncontrolled anger! You do *not* need anyone to tell you that you can out-drain your human spirit by *over*-reaction, *over*-thought, *over*-carefulness or overt-assumption; grumbling or complaining, when all you really needed to have done was to have studied *"to be quiet ..."* – well calmed, awaiting God to prove Himself!

In the heat of the battle, while looking for sympathy, you have squealed out vital information to enemy-agents sent to espy your battle-lines and formations. You have betrayed your spouse, your errant teenager, your silly employees, your un-wholesome family members, your lover; you have spoken un-advisedly with your lips. This is the sole cause of protracted delays and disappointments. You failed to realize the value and worth of your loved ones because you valued *your* uncontrollable burst of emotions more than they!

*You should have learned how to patiently wait on the Lord!*

## The Art of Waiting upon the Lord

Waiting upon the Lord is an *art!* It is not the engagement of a formula; a schemed-out, calculated, predetermined exercise to get you out of life's deep mires in order to gain ascendancy of the position of *your* pre-destination. That would be purely selfish in orientation. But even a far greater injustice done this *art* is the presumptuous notion *we* have held about it. Like an enthusiastic amateur painter, we pick the brush, dip it in a container of an expensive paint – and guess it; splodge blotted paint patches on the canvass.

No, painting is an *art*. A devoted artist patiently cultivates and develops his talent!

Most christian people were taught that *"waiting on the Lord"* connotes declaring a fast anyhow, anyway! So we fast and *not* pray! We fast and still curse, swear or use a strong language.

*So then how can we define "waiting" on the Lord?*

The *art* of waiting on the Lord commences as an individual's conscious perception and awareness of the Lord's presence with them while the Lord Himself is aware of their *tarrying at* His throne! At such a time as this, you are alone with God! Some other time however, we cannot *tarry* in the Throne Room because of a necessary demand upon our time; we may need to go to work or attend to little children, yet we know it too well that we needed to *wait upon the Lord!* At such occasions, we would need to cultivate the *art* of being in his presence!

Shepherd boy David did not have a fore-counsel of engaging Goliath in battle on the day they had met. He only ran an errand for his Dad: to see the welfare of his brothers at the battlefront. But anywhere David went, he always practiced the *art* of being in God's presence; he carried with him, the aura of the presence of God Almighty. On that fateful day Goliath confronted David, his head had fallen off his neck in a triumphant jubilation in the camp of the hitherto demoralized army of Israel! Thus, David was *un-armed*, yet ready; *un-prepared*; yet un-relenting!

Has not God said through Prophet Isaiah:

> *"But they that wait upon the LORD shall renew their strength; they shall mount up with wings as eagles; they shall run, and not be weary; and they shall walk, and not faint"?*
> Isaiah 40:31

Isaiah, in that verse quoted above used a word quite varied and extensive in meaning relating to the expectations of those that wait upon the LORD. Originally from the Hebrew word *'qavah'*, 'wait' carries with it the figurative expectation of a servant waiting upon his master, or a waiter readily waiting upon his/her guest's final choices as they order their menu!

'*Waiting*' therefore connotes any of these phrases: *"being banded together, wholly focused on collecting, gathering, expecting, looking out for patiently, tarrying for, waiting on or waiting upon!"*

When you wait upon the Lord, therefore, these eight most pronounced activities shall automatically be attendant in your life vis-à-vis: calmness in the Spirit, fasting associated with prayer, meditating upon God's word, speaking in tongues, witnessing about Christ and sharing testimonies.

Other activities that you would be involved in while you *wait upon the Lord* include verbalizing your victory, performing magnanimous acts of worship, offering sacrifices of worship and praise *en route* your victory.

Let us examine each, briefly!

*i.) Calmness of spirit:*
We see a perfect example of calmness of spirit and self-composure in Daniel – even after he had learned of the ploy of the members of the Babylonian Parliament to do away with his life! The Bible says:

> "*Now when David knew that the writing was signed, he went into his house; and his windows being open in his chamber toward Jerusalem, he kneeled upon his knees three times a day, and prayed and gave thanks before his God, as he did aforetime.*"
>
> Daniel 6:10

At this time Daniel was an aged man; about 80 years of age!

He had been in Babylon for over sixty years. Everybody including King Darius knew he had *"served God continually"* and that his God would deliver him.³

*Haven't you noticed that it is they, only, who had maintained a consistent walk with the Holy One of Israel who could maintain a spirit of calmness when trouble comes?*⁴

*ii.) Meditating upon God's Word:*
Joshua wrote:

> *"This book of the law shall not depart out of thy mouth; but thou shalt meditate there in day and night, that thou mayest observe to do according to all that is written therein: for then thou shalt make thy way prosperous, and then thou shalt have good success."*
>
> Joshua 1:8

The age-long subject of meditating in the Scriptures necessarily involves the art of *reading, studying, pondering, muttering, imagining, re-collecting, memorizing, talking about and ultimately applying scriptural principles to real life situations.* None of the nine component structure should be amiss for a wholesome meditation to be achieved.

*iii.) Speaking in Tongues:*
Paul wrote in *First Corinthians chapter fourteen, the second and fourth verses:*

> *"For he that speaketh in an unknown tongue speaketh not unto men, but unto God: for no man understandeth him; howbeit in the spirit he speaketh mysteries.*
>
> *He that speaketh in an unknown tongue edifieth himself ..."*

Speaking in tongues did not elapse with the Apostles of the Early Church, Satan would do all to have you convinced against this truth! The Bible informs that speaking in unknown tongue(s) is the easiest link you will establish with the Father to enable you *"charge up"* your spirit-man; speaking volumes to God in mysteries that even your mind cannot comprehend! Because of the routing via spirit-Spirit modem as it were, I can relax and *'blab'* in tongues under my breath while the next person to me is oblivious to my *'art.'*

Some other time, however, I have prayed violently in the Spirit – particularly at emergency occurrences.

July 2010, I had visited South Africa to assess our new ministry that was just being planted. On this particular occasion, our team comprising of the pastor, an elder and I came upon a fresh accident that had involved a nine year old boy and a lady motorist, on a highway of 60km/h zone, in the Blue Downs area of Capetown. The boy had dashed across the highway – and had been mowed down, head hit against the sidewalk, covered in a pool of blood! But the Holy Spirit motioned us to go raise him to life.

Obeying the Spirit's lead, we got off our car; knelt on the highway – traffic having built up on either side of the road, and did the bidding of God's Spirit. After eight minutes of praying in the Holy Spirit, I commanded life back into the lifeless body. He sneezed at first; then suddenly gasped for air before commencing a gradual but rhythmic breathing. Close to ninety motorists and pedestrians who had gathered to watch what was transpiring shouted for joy, still dazed in their unbelief because they were traditional ritualists!

At this point, the ambulance crew arrived and we surrendered the boy to them – having laid hands upon them, too, for God's wisdom to accompany them in the impending restorative task.

I flew out of Capetown the following day for England, but our team traced the victim out in the hospital; brought him gifts – and a special word of the Lord from myself. Today, Rashid is alive and well. Doctors confided in our team that they had never seen such a wholesome, quick recovery through a major surgery, before!

We give God all the praise!

The choice both of circumstances and mechanisms of praying in the spirit are entirely yours!

*iv.) Witnessing about Christ and Sharing Testimonies:*
The scripture says: *"The fruit of the righteous is a tree of life and he that winneth souls is wise."*[5]

Do you know what becomes of a rechargeable, cell-operated electrical appliance that is overcharged, and yet left un-used over time?

It retains 'full-charge' status for a while; then becomes a cold, dusty, under-utilized, malfunctioning, rusty, and short-circuited cell.

*Does this analogy describe you, presently?*

Listen. Do not short-circuit your productivity! Energy gained must be released to make maximum impact. What you do not use, you eventually loose; that is the way the Creator of life has so designed it.

Share testimonies; you may not know whose life you enriched if you did. Moreover, testimony sharing is *the* way to maintain *your* long term victory.⁶

I share testimonies quite often, and this has made either preaching to a crowd or witnessing to a soul quite easy for me. I do not need to *preach at* people before the Holy Spirit has begun His work of *convicting* or *confirming* the souls of men. Ever since I did ask the Lord to make my life testimonial did He really make not just my life, but my everyday life attest to His faithfulness! This has made witnessing about Him to others such a delightful experience for me!

*v.) Verbalizing your Victory, Every Time:*

> *"For verily I say unto you, That whosoever shall say unto this mountain, Be thou removed, and be thou cast into the sea; and shall not doubt in his heart, but shall believe that those things which he saith shall come to pass; he shall have whatsoever he saith."*
>
> Mark 11:23

When it seems as if you are loosing the battle, declare your victory! If your body proves un-well yet; dare stand upon God's promises and declare sound health. Before you leave for the interview location, declare your job or contract specification; pronounce your declarations over and over again. Remember, *whoever talks faith gets fit!*

*vi.) Offering Sacrifices of Worship and Praise:*

> *"Whoso offereth praise glorifieth me: and to him that ordereth his conversation aright will I show the salvation of God."*
>
> Psalms 50:23

Offering sacrifices of praise and worship – in the midst of turmoil – confuses the enemy. Worship and praise send earthquakes and thundering right to the headquarters of Satan. When Paul and Silas offered sacrifices of worship and praise at such an hour the devil thought he had placed a lid upon their lives, supernatural deliverance availed itself automatically – accompanied by earthquakes![7]

*vii.) Performing Magnanimous Acts:*

> *"Be not forgetful to entertain strangers: for thereby some have entertained angels unawares."*
>
> Hebrews 13:2

Be kind to visitors – and strangers. Never cast a high look at the less fortunate; for example, the refugees, the poor and the homeless. Do not oppress anyone. Rather relieve the oppressed. Visit the fatherless and the widows. Give alms – not to the lazy, unwilling-to- work, professional beggars, but the very poor!

If you put into practice these suggestions, your maximal profiting in delay will be undeniable.

## Chapter 8

# Overcoming Delays

*"Life is 10% what happens to you and 90% how you react to it."*

*- Charles R. Swindoll;*
*(U.S Clergyman, Author and Broadcaster)*

What Chuck Swindoll is saying in the above quote is this simple: your attitude determines whether you will lose or profit in life. God wants the best for you; so do I. I want you to profit from the adverse blows, delay has dealt you. I want you to win; and be triumphant despite your past.

In this chapter, I have shared with you principles on how to conquer some of the commonest delays in life which include general everyday delays; financial delays, procrastination and reproductive or conception delay.

*Shall we examine them each?*

## *Overcoming General Everyday Delays*

Charles Swindoll in his book *Living Above the Level of Mediocrity* rendered a long list of twenty-five things that would get you irritated. Among them were: *"Traffic jams, long queues, late planes, flat tires and cold foods."* I dare to add to his list a few things that would kill an enjoyable atmosphere for me; my additions include: *late meals, badly coordinated messages, ill-disciplined motorists and pedestrians, to say the least.*

These above are a few examples of ordinary daily delays which if wrongly reacted to, would give the enemy a beach-head from which to launch a major attack over destinies!

You will never overcome traffic jams in our mega cities for instance, by swearing at the driver of the car in front – or banging the driving wheel in a show of annoyance and impatience. Rather, I believe the tool-kit with which to deal with traffic congestion delays is found in one word: *adjustment!*

*Are you willing to adjust?*

Then:

- to overcome your *strong feelings* in a traffic jam, slot in the CD of a conference message/training you were yet to find time to listen to – and do listen to it;

- if you are going for an appointment or an interview, take along with you a book or colorful magazine of a completely un-related topic to the interview scenery! Your choice could be as varied as from sports to politics to religion, cookery, sewing *et cetera!* We do this in order to engage our waiting period, constructively enough!

Watch this: interviewers or future employers could swap your very interview questions round the very sign(s) of un-preparedness that your body language or insecure looks portray to them. So be confident, positive and smart!

*What am I trying to say?*

Do not waste *idle* time; invest it!

*The Navigators* with headquarters in Colorado, U.S.A had always centered their ministry upon encouraging youths of College and University age to carry on them packets of complimentary-sized cards, usually printed with embossed prints of memory verses to engage their *idle* times by. At canteen or bus queues, you could tell who they were when you saw them finger-waddling through rectangular packs of cards, lip-talking;

- to arrest late meals, prepare for a major adjustment! Go join your lady in the kitchen. Encourage her by engaging in *constructive* (not instructive) activities around the floor; activities like washing the dishes, basting the turkey and wrapping it in foil, cleaning the cabinet and worktop, mopping the floor – and the like!

Once in a while, organize a surprise reprieve for your wife – and children. Book a date for eating out in *her/their* favorite restaurant or eatery. Some other days, you issue her an order to not cook today because you are going to don the chef's garment and make the whole family *her* delicious meal you used to make her when you both started dating and courting!

I prophesy to you, that your wife, very soon would adjust, tenderly towards you, *if* you first become the *'paschal lamb'*, burden-bearer, leader-by-example in that home! (Your children too, who are learning by keen watchful observations will soon follow suit. That way, you would never raise a rebellious teen-ager: they know and are deeply assured of a father's love!)

## *Ten Tips to Overcoming Financial Delays*

Mismanagement of resources and endowments, indebtedness and lack of investment acumen are the greatest shackles militating against financial freedom!

*How do we smelt the chains of financial indebtedness?*

Let us engage these simple ten tips aimed at overcoming financial delays:

i.) *Develop the habit not to allow your spending exceed your income at any time.*

ii.) *Shop and ask around for the lowest quote – comparing interest rates from different lending giants – before committing yourself in mortgage deals or other loans. Like the popular motoring 'AA' advert says; "Just Ask!"*

iii.) *Resist the urge to apply for another credit card:*
Credit Card Companies will always tug at your wallet. They will employ every available means to woo you; your firm decision it must be not to fall for their *charms*!

Do *not* use a credit card to service the payment of an existing loan or indebtedness – unless this card guarantees you an un-chargeable, interest-free period during which you could reasonably reimburse your creditors!

*iv.) Practice much of denial of selfish cravings and thirst, at pressing moments:*
For instance if your custom it is to *down* a bottle of red, vineyard wine after a good meal, adjust onto drinking ordinary water for the period of time you need to balance your budget. This may not be an easy alternative at the onset, but with self discipline it would be found profitable.

*v.) Endeavor to cut your telephone bills – and energy bills at all cost:*
Do not allow the church's, company's or home telephone lines to be used indiscriminately. Not even authorized personnel, for instance, your secretary should be permitted to place frivolous or personal calls at the company's expense. Hence, you need to monitor and possibly reconcile your bills from time to time. Remember, even the billing communication companies are subject to errors!

In a house filled with buzzing teenagers, you may want to first consult with your breed on the idea of changing your line to "receive only" boxes or locked/coded receiver boxes if you cannot meet up with your monthly payments at present, before actually doing so.

Save energy, thus saving energy bills. Turn off un-used appliances. Choosing the "Standby" option still generates some power - and thus attracts some charges! Un-plug plugs from sockets. Switch off your gas boiler when it is warmer. Switch off monitors, laptops and personal computers. Switch off exhaust fans in the baths/restrooms once your tenure has expired. Switch off lights once you can see perfectly in the daytime. Use energy-saving bulbs.

Take cold showers on hot summer days – you will love its re-freshening feeling.

*vi.) Do not drive your car everywhere - particularly over walkable distances:*
Park your car – and take a stroll or ride a bicycle over manageable distances; you may be pleasantly surprised how much in need of muscle tuning you may be after a considerable time without physical exercise.

Take a stroll with your spouse. Go on a bicycle ride with him/her – or indeed with the whole family; there is a bonding that will evolve from shared activity such as this. I love in particular to share my oldest daughter's bicycle. Follow my advice: your bonding with your loved ones will be stronger, your muscles, firmer – along with your wallet!

*vii.) Schedule a repayment agreement with your creditors:*
Indebtedness worries, angers and depresses a lot of debtors! Your indebtedness may have arisen due to your *ex's* unscrupulous, financial ir-responsibility for which you were somehow, jointly liable! You may have got a divorce, but *his* debt is still with you. This may compound not just the accumulating interests but heart-aches and agonies.

Now you are tempted to give up altogether, pull the duvet over and sleep off your day; particularly in the wake of mounting interest charges being added to the original debt at every calendar month-end! Don't sleep on top of a mounting debt, instead, pull yourself together and move into action. Forgive yourself. Forgive the offender – and purpose to rise out of the ashes.

Never leave a debt alone – or it will not leave *you* alone!

Get debt advice; there is a governmental initiative in England to help overwrite from 75% to all of the money that you have been wrongly billed or which you cannot afford to repay, if you qualify for such an incentive. Visit your local Citizens Advice Bureau.

Call your creditor. Explain your financial situation at the time; most creditors will be glad to accept a minimum monthly re-payment that is reasonably agreeable to both parties. Schedule a re-payment agreement plan spread over a medium range period. Do not enter into a repayment agreement too long or short! Exercise financial prudence always!

*viii.) Keep a receipts and bills file:*
Find a lift-arch folder to safe-keep your receipts and invoices. Reconcile them monthly or quarterly as the case may warrant, to gain insight into which areas of spending needed more cuts or investments. This practice will help you to prepare your next financial forecast!

*ix.) Pay your tithes, offerings and vows to the Almighty God*:
A non-tither must surely live a mandated tight life.[1]

*x.) Plant faith-seeds:*
Sow regular 'faith seeds' into Kingdom work anytime there avails you an opportunity to do so. The principle of *"Seed-time & Harvest-time"* is the greatest back breaker whack to financial delays.[2]

## *Overcoming Procrastination*

Overcoming procrastination can only be achieved by overcoming bad time management! Simply, this means you would need to adjust your *'psychosomatic clock'* to attune to what needed being done for each day. This adjustment will indeed help organize your mind. If your mind is organized, your schedules would run smoother – and timelier!

Psychology experts notice that overcoming procrastination will ensure the battle being fought and won in the mind, as it is the engine of the body. For example, if you are going to work at 8 a.m., common sense – that may be uncommon – advises you to go to bed early, the night previous, shunning the temptation to watch a late night movie! You would necessarily need to climb into bed after the *prime time* news!

Additionally, you'd switch off the BlackBerry, mobiles/cell phones – and not forgetting Face Book appliances. Bed time is meant to traditionally be Bible read in bed, prayers said and lying down to rest a weary body!

If you are the *forgetful procrastinator*, prepare a daily itinerary, and with the help of magnetic holders, stick your itinerary on the refrigerator door, the dressing mirror, the back of the living room door, upon the rubber part of your car's steering wheel – or indeed, any other place(s) it would not escape your glance or attention. If you were tidier than I, you could nail upon a wall section of your kitchen, a cute *Notice Board*! Just ensure you asked your spouse's permission before doing so.

If you are the *lazy procrastinator*, get yourself connected to somebody who is a hard worker and a 'go-getter'. The aim is to give you a pull, a tug or the needed 'push' to forge on in life; into your productivity without you resenting them. I needed to say that you both possibly sign an agreement that you wouldn't resent their "push" before you got started!

If you are the *deep sleeper*, set an alarm clock placed on the shelf, a little farther than sleepy hands could reach in the early morning hours! Two mobile clock-alarms blaring strident and *undanceable* tunes, set five minutes apart, have always been more helpful to me!

If you are the *depressive procrastinator*, dig, unashamedly, to the very bottom your depression! Depressions have causes. You must know the root cause of your *downcast*. Elijah was a mighty man of God; he fell into the thick webs of depression after being issued a threat to his life by a Queen called Jezebel. The prophet of God ran more than a hundred miles in *self-preservative mode*, escaping from Jezebel's threat to behead him. Later when he had awoken from a deep rest in the wilderness of Beersheba, he had been more depressed, preferring death! When confronted by God why he'd chosen to act the way he'd acted, Elijah was forthright. He'd owned up!

Depression sprouts when you ignore, deny or totally dismiss with the wave of the hand or ignore the evident facts which your loved ones, sincere neighbors or people around you – who indeed are your mirrors – point to as signs of depression. Those signs at its onset will include:

i.) an unwillingness to wake up, get out of bed to face normal daily chores;
ii.) insomnia – lack of sleep at the right time of the night or very late into the *wee* hours of the morning;

*iii.)* deep, yet fruitless thoughtfulness and concern about your wasted living which you're powerless to change;
*iv.)* withdrawal and isolation from friends, families and loved ones to be alone in dark places;
*v.)* self harm;
*vi.)* irritability and petulance;
*vii.)* abstinence from nourishing foods and meals;
*viii.)* getting addicted or 'hooked up' on substances, gadgets or sex – or things that only yield temporary pleasure;
*ix.)* escapism and giving unreasonable excuses to avoid or discuss the obvious factual;
*x.)* an unhealthy dependence on family members to sort you out when you're of age – and able to sort yourself out;
*xi.)* disinterest in living a purposeful life – or in living altogether;
*xii.)* increasingly lonesome;
*xiii.)* disinterest in going to the house of the God to worship, and so on!

If you have noticed any of these symptoms present in your lifestyle, you may need the counseling of a psychiatrist or an appointment with your doctor!

On another hand, the root-cause of heavy suicidal depression may be an abuse witnessed or suffered – or a negative word spoken over a life at youth! At such times, a *"spirit of heaviness"* – usually a demon, and a gloomy cloud of darkness surround the victim. If your situation fits into my description, you would have noticed that your symptoms defy medications. This is because medical sciences cannot cure spiritual illnesses. Approach an anointed servant of God/ministry to "cast out" and uproot these evil, spiritual root-causes! Instead of demons that cause depression, God will now anoint your head with the "oil of gladness", and clothe you with a new "garment of praise."[3]

## *Overcoming Conception Delay*

I have deliberately chosen *not* to use either of the commoner phrases such as: *"Overcoming Infertility"* or *"Overcoming Barrenness."* Constructively engaging the use of positive terms of expression to describe yourself is the first spiritual and victorious approach you would need to consider adapting to and embracing. You must reject all negative human labels, at all cost.

Being positive may actually lead you and your spouse to consider adoption. This is scriptural, morally sound and legally upright. Queen Esther had been adopted and raised by her uncle, Mordecai, the Jew!

God may also be introducing you to a *blended family* – that is a family consisting of a single parent who had lost the other parent to death or divorce. *"God places the solitary in families and gives the desolate a home in which to dwell; He leads the prisoners out to prosperity; but the rebellious dwell in a parched land"* (Psalms 68:6-7).

Father God may also be laying on your heart to build an orphanage – or run an orphanage ministry. Remember, both orphans and widows command such a high attention before the eyes of the God of Heaven; ministering to them is more than rewarding!

Medically, you may also want to consider with your spouse the options of *IVF* treatments. Other ways to approaching delay in conception have been exhaustively treated in Hannah's story earlier on in *Chapter 6*.

## Chapter 9

# Virtues that Enable Maximal Profiting in Delay

*"I'm so glad to find a man who can go ahead without me!"*
*- (Abraham Lincoln; defending his choice of Ulysses Grant).*

When life is but over and nothing can be changed, whatever course of action you'd chosen to take or not take whilst you sojourned on earth will either be vindicated or condemned by the Word of God – and not the Word only, but also history!

Because of the veracity of the above statement, I simply cannot resist the urge to share basic virtues embossed in history, about ordinary men and women who had turned protracted and debilitating delays into blessings. Possibly by reading them, you too may take appropriate cues, and apply the necessary adjustments to your life. Reading of the accomplishments of such names as *Rosa Parks, Abraham Lincoln, Ulysses Simpson Grant* and *Winston Churchill* will doubtless add values to your life – both now and in preparation for eternity!

With the pleasure of rich hindsight and histories of such inestimable legacies left for us by men and women who conquered the giants of their times, I intend to summarize my discussions in this book.

Thus, in Rosa Parks, I found *resilience;* in Abraham Lincoln, *tolerance;* Ulysses G. Grant *persistence, endurance, ingenuity and self-confidence;* and in Sir Winston Churchill, *courage and conviction!*

Come with me down history lane!

## *Rosa Parks' 12 Year Resilience*

History forever reminds us of the Montgomery, Alabama 1955 Bus Boycott - aimed at de-segregating the Buses in the United States. In the eye of the hurricane was a 42 year old upright seam-mistress of the Montgomery Fair Department store named Rosa Parks!

The cruel Montgomery's segregation laws applied onto the Buses were fairly complex: African-Americans were mandated to pay their fare to the driver; then get off and re-board same bus through the back door! Sometimes the bus driver would deliberately drive off even before the paid-up customer had made their way to the rear entrance.

Not only this, if the white section was full and another white entered, African-Americans were required to give up their seats and move further to the back; a black person was not even allowed to sit across the aisle from whites. And yet 67% of bus riders in Montgomery were of African descent!

## The Making of Rosa Parks' Destiny

Mrs. Parks was not the first to have refused to give up her seat! Earlier, in the spring and October of same year, two other ladies: 15 year old Claudette Calvin and a young woman Mary L. Smith had contravened the law - and had been arrested. The local leaders of N.A.A.C.P (the National Association Against Cruelty and Prejudice) rejected them as appropriate vehicles! They were looking for someone more matured and able to withstand the scrutiny of the Courts and Media. So both ladies paid the fines and were released!

## The D-Day: Watch The Facts!

December 1, 1955 it was; in the closing rush hours! Rosa took a seat in the fifth row – the first row of the *"colors section."* The driver was the same one who had put Mrs. Parks off a bus twelve years earlier for refusing to get off and re-board through the back door: Rosa Park's delay period is thus easy to calculate.

*"The driver was still mean looking,"* she had been quoted as saying. Her sensibilities had been sharpened through participation in the NAACP's teaching of *"Don't frown, don't struggle, don't shout; don't pay the fine."* She knew more than precisely what to do when she was arrested!

The next day, a "ONE DAY STAY OFF BUS CAMPAIGN" was effected by all blacks in protest of the arrest and trial of Rosa Parks!

*"Please stay off the buses, Monday"* it read. And every black complied.

Meanwhile, Parks was scheduled to appear in court. She made her way through multitudes in the court house, a demure calm figure, fancifully and tastefully dressed, well composed. The trial lasted thirty minutes with the expected conviction and penalty. She was pronounced guilty!

That afternoon of Rosa's conviction, the Montgomery Improvement Association was formed with a relatively new comer to Montgomery, the young minister of *Dexter Avenue Baptist Church*: the Reverend Martin Luther King Jr.

This marked the beginning of the activist work of Dr. Martin Luther King Jr. and the beginning of the end of Alabama's *"crudest"* laws. On December 21, 1956; (a little more than a year in tense battle), Montgomery's Public Transportation system was legally integrated. Mrs. Park's resilience had paid off.

Dare to make a difference in *your* days?

## Abraham Lincoln's Tolerance of Ulysses S. Grant's Background during the American Civil War

When in April 1860 Northerner Abraham Lincoln was elected president of the United States, (with anti-slavery views); eleven Southern States (that traded in slavery and agricultural farmlands) voted to secede from the UNION; enraging the remaining twenty-two States at that time.

In April 1861, the first American civil war shots glowed from the barrels of guns and artilleries. But Ulysses Simpson Grant did not hope to lead an active military life! Born in 1822 in Ohio, son of a leather-merchant; he was a drunkard, a man who lacked purpose, so it seemed, at the earlier points of his life.

Ulysses had attended the *U.S. Military Academy at West Point, New York*. He was not even an ideal student; his list of misdemeanors was not at all short. Nevertheless, he graduated in 1843, day-dreaming to become a professor of Mathematics.

By 1845 – at age 23; he had fought with distinction in a U.S-Mexico War; yet he had quit the military shortly afterwards. He seemed restless! He tried farming and failed! He attempted real Estate business and that had also failed; infact, very woefully!

Still disillusioned, he embraced heavy drinking. However, his date with destiny was awaiting him, unbeknown to him. Many woes besieged him whom fate was destined to one day become the President of the United States of America!

## *Grant's Direction in fulfilling Destiny*

When the American civil war broke out, Grant counted upon his *West Point* qualification - and offered his services to fight for the *Northern Army* (as a Unionist). He was flatly rejected however! Despite battling with this bitter rejection, *something* kept urging him on: his persistent quality began to manifest! (That will be also be found true of you when you fight rejection of any kind with focus, determination and persistence.) Eventually, Grant secured command of an infantry regiment.

Then, he won rapid promotions!

In between the Civil War outbreak and March 1864, Abraham Lincoln had appointed and dismissed three

Commanding Generals! Numerous attempts to capture the Confederate Capital, Richmond in Virginia had failed, and kept failing! Grant on his part, ever since re-enlisting in the Army had conquered Shiloh; and by the end of 1862 had reached Vicksburg, a well fortified stronghold dominating the Mississippi. Attempted assaults on the city in the past had been unsuccessful. Grant's superiors in the Army were sure he would fail too!

Grant, unlike his predecessors, abandoned the experts' plan of attack, and through the in-born ingenuity found in people destined for the throne, embarked on his own risky, tasking and long campaigns. He and his men went through hard and thin, making advances on the enemy through forests and swamps. With the support of Union ships which had succeeded in steaming past Vicksburg; Grant transported his men across the Mississippi, worked his way up to Jackson and attacked Vicksburg from the East!

He *succeeded*.

May you too succeed!

## Lincoln's pressing Need: A Conqueror of Richmond!

To end the brutal civil war, Lincoln concluded that same confederate capital Richmond *must* be captured. He now faced the choice of appointing a new General Commander of the Union Forces!

> "It was a choice of a crude, lower-cadre, distinguished War fighter or one of the finest Superior Boardroom War planners" says Lincoln! Upon this single last choice of Lincoln's rested

the destiny of the United States of America! The President knew that too well, so he weighed his choice heavily; the scales, gently rocking!

Grant's opponents' viewpoints reached the President! The sage President however made his choice of Ulysses Simpson Grant public: *"I need this man; he fights! But I know how it's been with the rest of them all ..."* Lincoln accused his preceding choices of lacking self confidence and of being unwilling to assume responsibilities:

> *"As soon as I'd put a man in the commanding position of the Army, he'd come to me with a plan of the Campaign - and about as much say: 'Now I don't believe I can do it: but if you say so, I'll try it on and so put the responsibility of success or failure on me!*
>
> *It isn't so with Grant! I'm so glad to find a man who can go ahead without me!"*

## Richmond Fallen, Atlanta Taken, the Union Re-Established!

Grant proved his mettle – and his critics were proven wrong! The *Battle of Wilderness*, to capture Richmond was critical, prolonged and costly to both sides. Robert E. Lee was a formidable opponent. But Grant did indeed carry on without the President! The battle turned savage and bloody. A tip-turn event, which always had decided destinies came when the confederate troops accidentally shot their own Generals! Ranks had been broken. By April 2, 1865 Richmond had fallen to Grant. A week later, Robert Lee had little option but to surrender – and the American Civil War had ended.

Mere three years later, in 1868, Lincoln's tolerance of Grant's mediocre background had yielded the dividends of an emerging well-respected Unionist General, well acceptable enough to the public to occupy the White House.

Grant became the President of the United States. He had also won a second term!

Ulysses Simpson Grant could easily have remained an unknown and an undistinguished *country-side* businessman but God provided him a link to his destiny: Abraham Lincoln!

May God provide you a link to your destiny too!

## *Winston Churchill: Britain's Triumphant Voice in the Wilderness of World War II*

Winston Churchill was born into a lineage of aristocracy and leadership. His grand-father, the 17th century John Churchill commanded the Forces of Europe against France. His father, Lord Randolph was the Duke of Marlborough! Little Churchill knew very early he had a date with destiny.

## *Churchill's Background & Rise to Power*

Born November 30, 1874, Churchill's childhood education records were un-impressive. He was behind, and at the bottom of his class. At 18 however, he entered the *British Sandhurst Military Academy* – and a couple of years later fought in Cuba. By 21, he was in Bangalore, India where he joined his regiment.

- He soon dabbled into the Media – and was thus the Correspondent for the *Morning Post* in South Africa!

- At 25, he was elected a Member of the British Parliament; the youngest ever! Soon enough he would become the Home Secretary!

- Then began World War I. Churchill, 36, became the first Lord of the Admiralty. The survival of England was paramount to him. He instinctively developed a passion to fight.

## *Churchill's Ingenuity*

For four long years, the World War I raged on. The Germans had dug trenches which made it really hard for opposing Ground troops to transport both themselves and their supplies. Churchill's genius found an expression: he conceived an idea of a machine that could wobble-cross the trenches undeterred! *And thus, the first ever crude tank was born!*

## *Churchill's Misfortunes in Life*

During the World War, because of the Administration's mis-interpretation of Churchill's war logics, the 40 year old Lord of the Admiralty was dismissed from office. But the War dragged on, onto the summer and autumn of 1916! That paved the way for the arrival of a new Prime Minister, Lloyd George, who summoned Churchill back to Government as the "Minister of Munitions." It was while at this post his earlier invention, the Armored Tank, was quickly perfected.

And soon, after the Americans joined in the War, on the 11th hour, the 11th day, the 11th month of 1918, Germany was defeated – and World War I was over!

After the War I, Lloyd George, the Prime Minister, was out of power. Brits went onto the poll in a General Election. The hopeful Winston Churchill had thought to replace Lloyd George. But it was not his time yet: Churchill had just undergone appendicitis. He groaned not only physically but mentally, as he had lost the Elections.

Two years later, the new Prime Minister Stanley Baldwin summoned Churchill to join his Cabinet as the *Chancellor of the Exchequer*, the Office his father once held. Now at 50, while he was believed to have reached the peak of his carrier, Corporal Hitler of Germany was just arriving on the world scene.

When the Great Depression arrived in Britain, there also arrived yet a new government from which the dynamic and courageous Winston Churchill was excluded. Thence, for the next ten years preceding the World War II, Churchill wandered in the wilderness, out of office, a lonely, frustrated figure.

## *His 'Busy-ness' in Idleness*

Churchill retreated home: to his beautiful wife and kids. Friends around the world often paid him visits there! But more, he steadied his nerves by occupying his idle time profitably!

*What activities did he immerse himself in at this 'waiting' time?*

- He built with his own hands a large part of two cottages and an extensive garden wall;

- He took to painting – and even sold some of his works to make ends meet;

- He further developed himself: he wrote a monumental history on his hero and ancestor, The First Duke of Marlborough. That book was titled: *"MARLBOROUGH III."*

But even in this wilderness experience Churchill preferred to refer to as *"quiet retreat"*; he received first class information from the Capitals of the World un-availed to the Prime Minister of the day. World leaders and friends who knew his worth visited him in his solitude!

## *The Lonely Prophet's Voice*

Germany's new leader's policies were gradually being made clear to the world. Albert Einstein was exiled; the black ominous pogrom cloud was gathering. In Africa, Mussolini's troops crushed Ethiopia. Churchill raised his voice: *"GREAT BRITAIN MUST ARM!"* But it sounded much like a soliloquy from a drunk, sang off-beat!

In October of that year, world attention shifted onto the abdicating King Edward VIII who had decided to exchange his throne for his heart-throb: Mrs. Wallis Simpson, the following June. The Government fought against the marriage. Churchill, rallying the friends of the King stood by the decision of the bachelor King; the Government faced opposition. Churchill, convinced of imminent dangers felt the Prime Minister ought to arm Britain against the up-coming Nazis; and not the innocent lover King!

## *Churchill's Conviction*

Churchill kept brooding upon the situation of Europe and Germany's moves on the whole. He was convinced Great Britain must beef up arms! From his quiet retreat, he hollered out to the open world:

> "Great Britain must arm! We must oppose the Nazi regime with its prodigious arms so swiftly developing. I have watched this famous Island descending the stair case which leads to a dark gulf!
>
> Hitler has torn up the treaties and thrown it to our faces, Europe is fast approaching a climax; there will be an explosion and a catastrophe which no imagination can measure!
>
> How are we going to stop this war which seems to be moving towards us in so many ways?"

## Some of Churchill's 'Prophetic' Utterances Great Britain Ignored

Here are some of the prophetic utterances of the great late statesman Winston Churchill:

> "Poor England, leading a free, careless life day to day, pondering along the pathway which leads to a path ALL wanted to avoid!
>
> By all means, follow your path of peace, but do not close your eyes to the fact that we are entering into a corridor of deepening and darkening danger!"

Yet, nobody listened!

Churchill cautioned against entering into any pact with Hitler's Germany. He referred to Corporal Hitler as: *"A maniac, a ferocious genius; the repository and expression of the most villain utterance that has corroded the human race."*

Hitler was busy making agreements of "No War!" with the other European countries; an agreement he would later utterly breach. Austria's takeover was celebrated with fireworks in Berlin; Czechoslovakia's invasion was to follow; then Poland's! In August of 1939, Moscow and Hitler signed a pact never to war against each other; but you and I know better with the giftedness of hindsight!

Chamberlain had earlier been fooled into signing an Anglo-German Naval agreement of an *"everlasting peace"* with Hitler! With a wide smile, holding up the paper bearing the insignia of both he and Hitler and waving it at *his* crowd, he had said: *"Our two peoples will never go to war again!"* But on September 1, 1939, the war fore-told by Churchill commenced with the Polish takeover: World War II it would be known for eternity!

## *Churchill fulfills Destiny*

For ten years in political wilderness, now Winston Churchill's voice rings out! By the 11 o'clock deadline - Chamberlain had given Hitler to withdraw from Poland had elapsed with no resultant action, - Great Britain declared war on Germany! Churchill was brought back to his old post: the first Lord of the Admiralty at age 64! His days of shining are now to commence! He entered the room he had quitted in sorrow and pain twenty-five years earlier! A radio message was beamed across to all the Ships' masts:

*"Winston is back!"*

Confidence in the War government grew overnight! The missing *ingredient* had been added. But there would be a reduction in the *spice!*

Not too long Churchill had been heralded back into the House, Cromwall, an unpredictable, audacious but well respected M.P would address the House. Nobody could foretell the contents of his speech that he had recited without notes! He faced Chamberlain, squarely, and said:

> "You have sat too long here for any good you have been doing! Depart, I say, and let's have done with you! In the name of God; go!"

At the European front, all was still tranquil on May 9. The dawn of May 10, Hitler dealt the dreaded blow: He attacked Belgium and Luxembourg.

Desperate and in haste, the British people summoned Winston Churchill to the Buckingham Palace. It was a two minute journey from the Admiralty! Winston Churchill became the most remembered Prime Minister of Great Britain!

At the swearing in ceremony, he had said:

> "I was conscious of a profound sense of relief. I felt as if I were walking with destiny: and all my past life had been the preparation for this hour and for this time!"

## In Conclusion

Churchill became the first man-made honorary citizen of the United States of America. He was at this time the youngest of the British House of Parliament, yet its Father! He was a possessor of history, a redeemer of history and a maker of history!

I leave you with one of his memorable quotes that I have cherished all these years:

*"In War, Resolution*
*In Defeat, Defiance*
*In Victory, Magnanimity."*

Churchill fulfilled his destiny; may you fulfill yours!

## Chapter 10

# Make Peace With God: Possess Your Canaan!

*"None can less afford to delay than the aged sinner. Now is the time. Now or never. You have, as it were, one foot already in the grave. Your opportunities will soon be over. Strive then, I entreat you, to enter in at the strait gate."*
  - Archibald Alexander, U.S. Clergyman; 1772 – 1851

What Winston Churchill said he had felt when the baton of leadership of Great Britain was handed over to him at such a critical time was a profound sense of relief: occupying the niche that had been carved for him by destiny! At none other instance did he ever say that he had profound peace achieving, succeeding or excelling! Neither will you find peace in another but in putting your whole trust in the *"Prince of Peace"* (Isaiah 9:6).

*"Therefore being justified by faith, we have peace with God through our Lord Jesus Christ!"*
Romans 5:1

Nothing compares with God's peace freely accessible through a complete, uninhibited trust in the finished work of Christ upon the Cross of Calvary, where the precious blood of the Lamb of God had been shed.

Receive His peace today: N-O-W!

If you would want to accept Jesus as your personal Savior and LORD, say this simple prayer aloud:

*"Lord Jesus, nothing compares with your peace! I want to make peace with You now. I am tired of running and hiding. I am tired of turmoil – and the troubles that my sins have brought my way!*

*Save me. Wash me. Forgive me through the power in your shed blood. Make me wholly yours! Write my name in the Book of Life; in Jesus' matchless name.*

*Amen!"*

If you just prayed that prayer with sincerity and faith in your heart, please contact me at:

*Sammy Joseph Ministries*
*Box 15129, Birmingham, England, B45 5DJ*
*twitter: SammyOJoseph*
*facebook: Sammy O Joseph*
*email: reverendsammy@harvestways.org*
*text/call: +44 7854675159 / 7906441276*

I would personally love to hear from you – so as to pray and rejoice with you.

May the Lord bless and keep you; may He make His face to shine upon you – and give you His peace, now and forever more. Amen.

# References

**Chapter 1**
1. *Psalms 90:12*
2. *Genesis 2:7*
3. *Psalms 36:9*
4. *2 Samuel 23:4*
5. *Isaiah 60:19-20*
6. *1Peter 1:24; NEB*
7. *Psalms 144:4*
8. *Cf. 2 Samuel 23:4*
9. *Joel 3:14*
10. *John 10:10*
11. *1 Peter 2:25*

**Chapter 2**
1. *Psalms 103:7; Exodus 2:1-10*
2. *Isaiah 14:27*
3. *Numbers 14:22*
4. *Nahum 1:2-3*
5. *Genesis 16:3; 31:7 & Revelations 2:10*
6. *Psalms 68:6*
7. *Hoshea 11:4, NIV.*
8. *Galatians 1:21b*
9. *2 Samuel 6:14-15*
10. *Ephesians 6:2*
11. *Habakkuk 2:3*
12. *John 3:8*
13. *2 Samuel 6:20*
14. *Jeremiah 31:32*
15. *Romans 11:16-25*
16. *Job 2:9*
17. *Genesis 11:31-32*
18. *1 Chronicles 22:8*
19. *1 Chronicles 22:14*
20. *Judges 21:6*

21. *Psalms 133:1-3*
22. *Proverbs 1:32; The Jewish Publication Society; (JPS Copyrighted.)*
23. *Jeremiah 31:15*
24. *Isaiah 39:1-8*

**Chapter 3**
1. *Genesis 12:6-9*
2. *Genesis 12:3-4*
3. *Genesis 20:13*
4. *Numbers 14:33 & 2 Kings 9:22*
5. *Romans 13:12*
6. *Hebrews 2:2*
7. *3 John 2*
8. *1Timothy 6:12*
9. *Proverbs 23:5*
10. *Joshua 7:1-26*
11. *Proverbs 13:11*
12. *Haggai 1:6*
13. *Hoshea 8:7*
14. *Deuteronomy 23:19*
15. *1Timothy 5:24-25*
16. *Genesis 31:6-9*
17. *Job 5:21*
18. *Proverbs 30:15-16*
19. *Psalms 102:19-20*

**Chapter 4**
1. *Numbers 14:9*
2. *Numbers 13:22*
3. *Numbers 13:28*
4. *Numbers 13:32*
5. *Numbers 14:4*
6. *Numbers 14:37-38*
7. *Psalms 105:15*
8. *Deuteronomy 2:3*
9. *Exodus 5:1*
10. *Psalms 127:3*
11. *Cf. Ephesians 6:4*
12. *Cf. Isaiah 45:10*
13. *2 Samuel 6:6-7*

14. Ber Translation of the Holy Bible
15. Genesis 31:19; 32
16. Leviticus 6:1-5
17. Judges 4:17-18
18. Judges 4:19
19. Luke 1:41
20. Song of Solomon 5:2-16
21. Haggai 1:3-11
22. 1 Corinthians 7:4-5

**Chapter 5**
1. Joshua 14:14 & 15:54-55
2. The correct answer is the last bullet point option.
3. 1 Samuel 25:3; Amplified Version.
4. 1 Samuel 25:3
5. 1 Peter 3:4
6. 1 Samuel 25:37
7. 1 Samuel 18:14
8. 1 Samuel 18:29 ; emphasis, mine.
9. 2 Samuel 6: 20-23
10. Proverbs 11:14
11. 1 Samuel 24:4-16 & 26:6-9
12. Psalms 39:1
13. 1 Samuel 25:29
14. 1 Samuel 25:5 & 38
15. Acts 9:16
16. Genesis 37:3
17. Genesis 37:4
18. 1 Samuel 9:14-16
19. Genesis 37:11
20. Luke 2:51
21. Genesis 37:25
22. Amos 6:1-7
23. 1 Samuel 13: 4-14
24. Numbers 3:4
25. Hebrews 10:29
26. Joel 3:3
27. Genesis 25:29-34
28. Matthew 26:14-16
29. Jeremiah 30:7
30. Genesis 34:2

[31.] *Genesis 39:3*
[32.] *1 Corinthians 2:9*

**Chapter 6**
[1.] *Malachi 3:10-11*
[2.] *Genesis 8:21-22*
[3.] *Genesis 6:1-6*
[4.] *Genesis 6:6, Amplified Version*
[5.] *Habakkuk 2:17*
[6.] *Psalms 16:11*
[7.] *1 Samuel 1:6*
[8.] *Acts 11:28*
[9.] *Acts 12:2*
[10.] *Acts 12:12*
[11.] *Acts 13:5*
[12.] *Acts 13:39*
[13.] *Galatians 2:7-9*
[14.] *Revelation 16:13; rendition, mine.*
[15.] *Acts 15:30-31*
[16.] *1 Kings 19:19-21; Galatians 2:2*
[17.] *John 1:19-36*
[18.] *Galatians 2:2 & 9*
[19.] *Acts 15:12*
[20.] *Acts 15:26*
[21.] *Cf. Acts 11:19-20; Galatians 2:11*
[22.] *Acts 4:36*
[23.] *Acts 1:23-26*
[24.] *Acts 15:34-35*
[25.] *Acts 6:3-4*
[26.] *1 Corinthians 14:33*
[27.] *Luke 5:8*
[28.] *Luke 5:11*
[28.] *Psalms 46:10-11; emphasis, mine.*
[29.] *1 Samuel 30:1-6*
[30.] *Philippians 4:2-3.*
[31.] *Acts 16:35-3*
[32.] *2 Timothy 1:5*

**Chapter 7**
[1] *Psalms 106:33*
[2] *Psalms 46:10*
[3] *Daniel 6:16*
[4] *Psalms 112:7-8*
[5] *Proverbs 11:30*
[6] *Revelations 12:11*
[7] *Acts 16:25-26*

**Chapter 8**
[1] *Malachi 3:8-10*
[2] *Genesis 8:22*
[3] *Isaiah 61:3*

# Other Books by the Author

Other books by the author that can be ordered at all Christian bookshops near you, *Pulse Publishing House* or from our website *www.harvestways.org* include:

## GIDEON:
## RELEASING THE POTENTIALS WITHIN YOU

This book draws analogies from the life of Gideon (one of Israel's Judges) and applies them to how you can effectively release the hidden potentials within you. Written in easy, straightforward, simple language, you will find basic practical insights that will help lift you above common mediocrity levels in life!
*(176 pages)*

## BEFORE YOU STEP INTO SOMEONE ELSE'S SHOES

This book contains *easy-to-do* guides on how you will not repeat the costly mistakes made by others faced with a fresh opportunity to begin anew after suffering a heavy setback. We have also provided essential checklists to anyone willing to *step into shoes* ordained of God for them – as well as checkmating the mutineers.
*(46 pages)*

Download *PULSE On-line*, freely at *www.harvestways.org*

# Worship with Us

**The Harvestways Int'l Church,
(Birmingham, U.K.)**
Holloway Community Hall
Northfield, Birmingham,
England, United Kingdom
B31 1TT
Sundays: 12 noon- 2pm
Fridays: 7–8.30pm (House Fellowship)
Tel: (+44) 7906441276 / (+44) 7854675159

**The Harvestways Int'l Church
(Nigeria, West Africa)**
1 Harvest Way, Off Elewura Street
Behind Zartech / GLO Office,
Challenge G.P.O Box 2910
Dugbe, Ibadan Oyo State,
Nigeria, West Africa.
Sundays: 9am
Wednesdays: 6pm
Mobile: (+234) 8078198576 / (+234) 8132360850

**The Harvestways Int'l Church
(Capetown, South Africa)**
Eindhoven School Hall
Eindhoven Delft South 7100
Capetown,
South Africa
Sundays: 9am – 11am
Wednesdays: 6pm
Mobile: (+27) 7436 55011 / (+27) 732454884
(+27) 219550776

You may want to inquire about SJM, invite Rev. Sammy to minister for you or become a partner; please contact:

Sammy Joseph Ministries
P.O. Box 15129,
Birmingham,
West Midlands,
England
B45 5DJ
twitter: SammyOJoseph
facebook: Sammy O Joseph
email: reverendsammy@harvestways.org
Mobile: (+44) 7906441276 / (+44) 7854675159

# Contact Addresses

**United Kingdom**
The Harvestways Int'l Church
@ Holloway Hall, Ley Hill
Birmingham
England
B31 1TT
or
Sammy Joseph Ministries
Box 15129
Birmingham,
England,
U.K
B45 5DJ
Tel: (+44) 7906441276 / (+44) 7854675159

**Nigeria**
Pulse Publishing House
Plot 1, Harvest Way
Behind GLO Office
Challenge
G.P.O. Box 2910
Dugbe
Ibadan
Nigeria.
Mobile: (+234) 8136812070/(+234) 8132360850

**South Africa**
Pulse Publishing House
351 Delft Main Road
Delft South
Capetown
South Africa
7100
Mobile: (+27) 7436 55011 / (+27) 732454884

*On-line availability @ www.harvestways.org, WHSmith.co.uk & Barnesandnoble.com*

# Notes

www.ingramcontent.com/pod-product-compliance
Lightning Source LLC
LaVergne TN
LVHW041614070426
835507LV00008B/236